A PLUME BOOK

THE INSPIRATIONAL ATHEIST

BUZZY JACKSON is the author of the award-winning *A Bad Woman Feeling Good: Blues and the Women Who Sing Them* and *Shaking the Family Tree: Blue Bloods, Black Sheep, and Other Obsessions of an Accidental Genealogist*. She has a PhD in history from the University of California, Berkeley, and is a correspondent for the *Boston Globe*. She lives in Colorado with her family and a freethinking dog named Ralph.

Among the many quotations her research revealed to be fictitious, her favorite was this one:

"Everything you see before you, I owe to spaghetti."
—(Not) Sophia Loren

THE
INSPIRATIONAL
ATHEIST

*Wise Words on the Wonder and
Meaning of Life*

COMPILED AND EDITED BY
BUZZY JACKSON

A PLUME BOOK

PLUME
Published by the Penguin Group
Penguin Group (USA) LLC
375 Hudson Street
New York, New York 10014

USA | Canada | UK | Ireland | Australia | New Zealand | India | South Africa | China
penguin.com
A Penguin Random House Company

First published by Plume, a member of Penguin Group (USA) LLC, 2014

P REGISTERED TRADEMARK—MARCA REGISTRADA

LIBRARY OF CONGRESS CATALOGING-IN-PUBLICATION DATA
The inspirational atheist : wise words on the wonder and meaning of life / compiled
and edited by Buzzy Jackson.
pages cm
"A Plume book."
ISBN 978-0-14-218142-3
1. Life—Quotations, maxims, etc. I. Jackson, Buzzy, compiler.
BD431.I57 2014
128—dc23
2014031219

Printed in the United States of America
1 3 5 7 9 10 8 6 4 2

Set in Granjon LT Std.
Designed by Eve Kirch

The author will donate a portion of her proceeds from *The Inspirational Atheist* to
the charitable organization Doctors Without Borders.

Dedicated to Gary Morris:
Friend, Agent, Wit, Mensch

CONTENTS

INTRODUCTION
CHICKEN SOUP FOR THE SOULLESS

From the mystery of the vast night sky to the sweet return of birdsong in the spring, our universe is filled with wonders we have only just begun to explore and understand. I've always found inspiration in the beauty of nature, in relationships with people I love and admire, and in the art and culture of the world around me. And while I've discovered plenty of inspiration in libraries and bookstores, it's never been in the "Inspirational" sections, because amidst all the shelves of "inspirational" books, I never encountered a single one that spoke directly to those of us with a secular outlook. Where, I wondered, was the book that collected and reinforced the feeling of awe we feel contemplating the cosmos and our place in it, our amazement at the puzzle of life itself, for those who are not religious? Where was the motivating quote of the day for nonbelievers?

Where, I wondered, was the *Chicken Soup for the Soulless*?

Here, I hope.

We all need a little inspiration now and then—and that

includes the atheists, the skeptics, the agnostics, and the "spiritual-but-not-religious" among us. You know who you are: As of 2012, one-fifth of the American public claims no religious affiliation at all, and we're growing in numbers each year across the Western world. As historian Jennifer Michael Hecht writes, "The earliest doubt on historical record was twenty-six hundred years ago, which makes doubt older than most faiths. Faith can be a wonderful thing, but it is not the only wonderful thing."

The Inspirational Atheist is for the growing population of humanists who believe that life has meaning when we live it meaningfully. Freethinking people are drawn to the secular humanist worldview because of the intellectual freedom *and* the ethical responsibility it demands. Nonbelievers do not practice kindness because some mythical figure tells us to; we do good because it is the right thing to do. *The Inspirational Atheist* is a book of wonderful things. And even more than that: a book of hundreds of revelations in which no one goes to Hell.

Because there is no Hell.

"Things are the way they are in our universe," wrote astronomer Brian Greene, "because if they weren't, we wouldn't be here to notice." And since we are here and we are able to notice, the effort we make to understand and appreciate our universe is surely one of humanity's highest callings. We can trace that effort to understand back at least forty thousand years to the prehistoric art of cave paintings. In those handprints and hunting scenes our ancient ancestors first distinguished themselves by choosing to interpret the world around them and not merely survive in it. That spirit of inquiry and irrepressible human curiosity led us tens of thousands of years from the caves of El Castillo and Chauvet to the human-made mountains of the Egyptian pyramids, from the massive force and mysteries of Stonehenge and Easter Island through the doomed frescoes of Pompeii and on to Galileo's delicate sketches of the moon viewed by telescope for the first time, and eventually to the breathtaking image of Neil Armstrong's first footprint on the lunar soil in 1969. Those ochre-spattered handprints on dark cave walls point directly to the stark gray footprint on the moon's Sea of Tranquility, an unbroken line of human creativity and exploration, forty thousand years of seeking to understand the universe and our place in it. And just as those handprints survived tens of thousands of years in the darkness, so our human footprints will remain on the surface of the moon for millions, perhaps billions of years, with no earthly breeze to erase them.

The quotations collected here are reflections on this quest and a reminder of that journey. What has always set freethinkers apart is their willingness to see the world as it is, not as they wish it to be. And it is this courage and this tradition of truth seeking that are responsible for humanity's singular stature on planet Earth. This book brings together some of humanity's greatest insights on the subjects that all people, faithful or not, return to in times of joy, stress, and challenge, and assembling them together as one collection helps us appreciate the common values we share. It's a feeling expressed by the poet Archibald MacLeish in 1968, when the Apollo 8 mission brought back the first photos humans had ever seen of Earth viewed from space. "To see the earth as it truly is, small and blue and beautiful in that eternal silence where it floats," wrote MacLeish, "is to see ourselves as riders on the earth together, brothers on that bright loveliness in the eternal cold—brothers who know now they are truly brothers." And sisters, of course.

Not everyone quoted in this book is an avowed atheist. But every bit of wisdom here can inspire us—all of us—to appreciate our world as we strive to understand it. Care has been taken not to include people whose religious faith was the defining aspect of their identity, so while I continue to be inspired by the words and actions of many people of faith including, for example, Dr. Martin Luther King, Jr.; Dietrich Bonhoeffer; Sojourner Truth; and Simon Wiesenthal, they and many others are not included here out of respect for their religious commitments.

It's easy for believers to find their fellows in faith; that's why organized religions organized in the first place. But the nonreligious are by nature independent, which makes it more challenging for freethinkers to find their philosophical sisters and brothers. *The Inspirational Atheist* is an attempt to help create that sense of community, and as this book reveals, it is a community that has existed for thousands of years, spanning all the Earth's continents. "Mortal men subsist by change and transference by one to the other," wrote Lucretius in the first century BCE, "and in a short space of time, the tribes of living creatures are changed by successive generations, and, like the racers, deliver the torch of life from hand to hand." We need one another, as Lucretius wrote, not only for love and affection, but in this great human project, passing on the torch of life from hand to hand, hoping to advance the cause of human understanding. As nonbelievers, we look to our fellow humans and not to the supernatural for support and inspiration. Isaac Newton, one of history's greatest geniuses, wrote that "if I have seen further, it is by standing on ye shoulders of giants"; his own scientific discoveries were built on the work of those who came before him. No man or woman, however brilliant, can hope to understand the mysteries of the universe alone.

The Inspirational Atheist is ultimately intended not as a strident call to arms against religion but as a rationalist's sincere invitation to optimism and wonder. While some books may emphasize the "a" in atheism—"without"—*The Inspirational Atheist* emphasizes what atheists have *with* them all the time: the rarefied sensitivity of the noticer, the appreciator, the *creator* of the good and the beautiful. We create the beauty in a flower by noticing and appreciating it is there. Much like *Homo sapiens*, flowering plants have only existed on Earth for a relatively short time. Yet among all living things on Earth we humans are perhaps the only species able to appreciate and even re-create a flower's beauty in a painting or drawing, something we've been doing for thousands of years. These acts give meaning to our existence . . . and we are born with that power.

Iris Murdoch once observed, "People from a planet without flowers would think we must be mad with joy the whole time to have such things about us." It's my hope that the thoughts collected here will remind every reader of the amazing privilege we all share of waking up in this universe, noticing the flowers, and creating lives of meaning every day.

THE
INSPIRATIONAL
ATHEIST

Advice

You are what you settle for.   —Janis Joplin

This is what you shall do: love the earth and sun and the animals, despise riches, give alms to every one that asks, stand up for the stupid and crazy, devote your income and labor to others, hate tyrants, argue not concerning God, have patience and indulgence toward the people, take off your hat to nothing known or unknown or to any man or number of men . . . re-examine all you have been taught at school or church or in any book, dismiss what insults your own soul, and your very flesh shall be a great poem.
                    —Walt Whitman, *Leaves of Grass*

Do not destroy what you cannot create.   —Leó Szilárd

Facing it, always facing it, that's the way to get through. Face it.   —Joseph Conrad, *Typhoon*

Humility is the mother of giants. One sees great things from the valley; only small things from the peak.
 —G. K. Chesterton, *The Innocence of Father Brown*

Stay sane.

—GALILEO GALILEI, writing to a colleague after being forced to retract his scientific observations by the Inquisition

Be fully awake to everything about you & the more you learn the more you can appreciate & get a full measure of joy & happiness out of life. I do not think a young fellow should be too serious, he should be full of the Dickens some times to create a balance.
 —LeRoy Pollock, in a letter to his son Jackson

Fast, Cheap, and Good . . . pick two. If it's fast and cheap, it won't be good. If it's cheap and good, it won't be fast. If it's fast and good, it won't be cheap.
 —Tom Waits, paraphrasing Jim Jarmusch

Listen to no one's advice except that of the wind in the trees. That can recount the whole history of mankind.
 —Claude Debussy

We are what we repeatedly do. Excellence, then, is not an act, but a habit. —WILL DURANT

Beware the barrenness of a busy life. —SOCRATES

Don't EVER EVER EVER bother to go on a diet. . . . Just be you & get on with it, I cannot tell you how much time & energy you'll save & how much happier you'll be. —EMMA THOMPSON, in a letter to her sixteen-year-old self

You practice and you get better. It's very simple. —PHILIP GLASS

Think like a man of action; act like a man of thought. —HENRI BERGSON

The only teacher I had in college that ever gave us writers good advice said, "Run five miles every day and take aspirin." The logic being that you're going to be in your 40s by the time you have anything worthwhile to say, and to just be alive by the time that comes. And that turned out to be very solid advice that I never followed. Solid as a rock. —JOHN JEREMIAH SULLIVAN

The best time to plant a tree was twenty years ago; the second best time is now. —CHINESE PROVERB

Don't just be yourself. Be all of yourselves. Don't just live.... Be life. —Joss WHEDON

Leap and the net will appear. —ANONYMOUS

Don't undertake a project unless it is manifestly important and nearly impossible.
—EDWIN LAND (inventor of the
Polaroid camera in 1947)

Write them. —MARLENE DIETRICH, on love letters

There is no mistake so great as the mistake of not going on.
—WILLIAM BLAKE (attributed)

Do those things that incline you toward the big questions, and avoid the things that would reduce you and make you trivial. —GEORGE SAUNDERS

Never pass up a chance to have sex or appear on television. —GORE VIDAL

Lots of people will tell you to follow your bliss: "Seek your passions, and money will follow." This is true, but impractical. When you are starting out almost no one knows what their passions are, and you become paralyzed because you can't give your all until you find your passion. A better strategy is to forget your bliss and to find your passion by mastering *something*, almost anything. As you master some skill, giving your 100% to it, you will inevitably move toward your passion, step by step, all the while earning a living. Most likely it will take all your life to find your bliss. So don't wait for your passion. Just master something. —KEVIN KELLY

Read everything and be kind.

—PENN JILLETTE

Quit now, you'll never make it. If you disregard this advice, you'll be halfway there. —DAVID ZUCKER

Never take advice from anybody. —ROBERT ALTMAN

Dare to be naïve. —R. BUCKMINSTER FULLER

When you are in the last ditch, there is nothing left but to sing. —SAMUEL BECKETT

What we bear is not so important as how we bear it. —STOIC MAXIM

First answers are usually knee-jerk. Second answers tend to be cute. Third answers to the same question sometimes tell the truth. —STEWART BRAND

It is almost impossible to overestimate the unimportance of most things. —JOHN LOGUE

Next time somebody tells you that something is true, why not say to them: "What kind of evidence is there for that?" And if they can't give you a good answer, I hope you'll think very carefully before you believe a word they say.

—RICHARD DAWKINS, in a letter to his ten-year-old daughter

Artists work best alone. . . . Work alone.

—STEVE WOZNIAK

We cannot regard the future of the civilized world in the same way as we see our personal futures. It is careless to be cavalier about our own death. It is reckless to think of civilization's end in the same way.

—JAMES LOVELOCK

My advice is to do what you can this second. Big plans that rely on other people, new equipment, long periods of time . . . they're no good. What can you do right now?

—MIRANDA JULY

Gentlemen, in the little moment that remains to us between the crisis and the catastrophe, we may as well drink a glass of champagne. —PAUL CLAUDEL

Empty your mind, be formless, shapeless—like water. Now you put water in a cup, it becomes the cup; you put water into a bottle it becomes the bottle; you put it in a teapot it becomes the teapot. . . . Be water, my friend.
—BRUCE LEE

We have to stop CONSUMING our culture. We have to CREATE culture. —TERENCE MCKENNA

It is better to have a permanent income than to be fascinating.
—OSCAR WILDE, *The Model Millionaire*

Seek not the paths of the ancients; Seek that which the ancients sought.
—MATSUO BASHŌ, "Words by a Brushwood Gate"

Eat the present moment and break the dish.
—EGYPTIAN PROVERB

Whatever you think can't be done, somebody will come along and do it. A genius is the one most like himself.
—THELONIOUS MONK

The best thing one can do when it is raining is to let it rain.
> —HENRY WADSWORTH LONGFELLOW, "The Poet's Tale;
> The Birds of Killingworth"

Understand that being able to say, "I don't know what to do with my life" is an incredible privilege that 99% of the rest of the world will never enjoy. —CHRIS WARE

Be a philosopher, but amidst all your philosophy, still be a man. —DAVID HUME

Only an amateur answers his critics. Read the bad reviews once, the good ones twice, and put them all away and never look at them again. —JOHN WATERS

Many of life's failures are people who did not realize how close they were to success when they gave up.
> —THOMAS EDISON

The secret of all victory lies in the organization of the non-obvious. —MARCUS AURELIUS

Do not fear mistakes, there are none. —MILES DAVIS

Try to be one of the people on whom nothing is lost.
> —HENRY JAMES

Begin to live at once, and count each separate day as a separate life.   —SENECA

Never pay the slightest attention to what a company president ever says about his stock.   —BERNARD BARUCH

Always do what you are afraid to do.

—RALPH WALDO EMERSON

Solvitur ambulando. (It is solved by walking.)
                                                        —DIOGENES

Nothing great was ever achieved without enthusiasm.
                                    —SAMUEL TAYLOR COLERIDGE

The chief danger in life is that you may take too many precautions.   —ALFRED ADLER

There is more danger in a violence that you don't face, when you continue to remain locked in a room with it.
                                              —MICHAEL ONDAATJE

Be less curious about people and more curious about ideas.   —MARIE CURIE

I have found that the best way to give advice to your children is to find out what they want and then advise them to do it. —HARRY S. TRUMAN

Always remember: If you're alone in the kitchen and you drop the lamb, you can always just pick it up. Who's going to know? —JULIA CHILD

Nobody cares if you can't dance well. Just get up and dance. Great dancers are great not because of their technique, they are great because of their passion. —MARTHA GRAHAM

You must do the thing you think you cannot do. —ELEANOR ROOSEVELT

I used to think as I looked at the Hollywood night, "there must be thousands of girls sitting alone like me, dreaming of becoming a movie star. But I'm not going to worry about them. I'm dreaming the hardest." —MARILYN MONROE

Art and Creativity

The only things in my life that compatibly exist with this grand universe are the creative works of the human spirit.
—ANSEL ADAMS

I can very well do without God both in my life and in my painting, but I cannot, ill as I am, do without something which is greater than I, which is my life—the power to create.
—VINCENT VAN GOGH

To me, literature is a calling, even a kind of salvation. It connects me with an enterprise that is over 2,000 years old. What do we have from the past? Art and thought. That's what lasts. That's what continues to feed people and give them an idea of something better.
—SUSAN SONTAG

My future starts when I wake up every morning. . . . Every day I find something creative to do with my life.
—MILES DAVIS

Inspiration is necessary in poetry as in geometry.

—ALEKSANDR PUSHKIN

Remember: information is not knowledge; knowledge is not wisdom; wisdom is not truth; truth is not beauty; beauty is not love; love is not music; music is the best.

—FRANK ZAPPA, "Packard Goose"

You never have to change anything you got up in the middle of the night to write.   —SAUL BELLOW

Drama is very important in life: You have to come on with a bang. You never want to go out with a whimper. Everything can have drama if it's done right. Even a pancake.   —JULIA CHILD

All that is worth remembering in life, is the poetry of it.

—WILLIAM HAZLITT

The secret of a man who is universally interesting is that he is universally interested.

—WILLIAM DEAN HOWELLS

My idea is that there is music in the air, music all around us; the world is full of it, and you simply take as much as you require.   —EDWARD ELGAR

The greater the artist, the greater the doubt. Perfect confidence is granted to the less talented as a consolation prize.   —ROBERT HUGHES

I suspect that one of the reasons we create fiction is to make sex exciting.   —GORE VIDAL

If you love what you do and are willing to do what it takes, it's within your reach. And it'll be worth every minute you spend alone at night, thinking and thinking about what it is you want to design or build. It'll be worth it, I promise.   —STEVE WOZNIAK

I occasionally have an anti-Roth reader in mind. I think, "How he is going to hate this!" That can be just the encouragement I need.   —PHILIP ROTH

The man who can't visualize a horse galloping on a tomato is an idiot.   —ANDRÉ BRETON

Much of good science—and perhaps all of great science—has its roots in fantasy.   —E. O. WILSON

Congratulate yourselves if you have done something strange and extravagant and broken the monotony of a decorous age.   —RALPH WALDO EMERSON

One should photograph objects, not only for what they are, but for what else they are.

—MINOR WHITE

There is an incessant influx of novelty into the world, and yet we tolerate incredible dullness.

—HENRY DAVID THOREAU

My sole inspiration is a telephone call from a producer.

—COLE PORTER

The aim of an artist is not to solve a problem irrefutably, but to make people love life in all its countless, inexhaustible manifestations.

—LEO TOLSTOY

Imagination is a force that can actually manifest a reality. . . . Don't put limitations on yourself. Other people will do that for you. Don't do that to yourself. Don't bet against yourself.

—JAMES CAMERON

If you've worked hard and kept your nose to the grindstone, something happens: The body gets old but the creative mechanism is refreshed, smoothed and oiled and honed. That is the grace. That is the splendid grace.

—MAURICE SENDAK

Words are, of course, the most power-ful drug used by mankind.

—RUDYARD KIPLING

Imaginative literature . . . does not enslave; it liberates the mind of man. Its truth is not like the canons of orthodoxy or the irrationality of prejudice and superstition. It begins as an adventure in self-discovery and ends in wisdom and humane conscience.　　　—CHINUA ACHEBE

History repeats itself, but the special call of an art which has passed away is never reproduced. It is as utterly gone out of the world as the song of a destroyed wild bird.
　　　—JOSEPH CONRAD, *The Mirror of the Sea*

Nothing attracts me like a closed door. I cannot let my camera rest until I have pried it open.
　　　—MARGARET BOURKE-WHITE

There is no theory. You have only to listen. Pleasure is the law.　　　—CLAUDE DEBUSSY

There is not a single true work of art that has not in the end added to the inner freedom of each person who has known and loved it.　　　—ALBERT CAMUS

The increase of known truths stimulates the investigation, establishment, and growth of the arts; not their diminution or destruction.　　—GALILEO GALILEI

Music is the effort we make to explain to ourselves how our brains work. We listen to Bach transfixed because this is listening to a human mind.　　—LEWIS THOMAS

The [Chauvet cave] rock paintings were made where they were so that they might exist in the dark. They were for the dark. They were hidden in the dark so that what they embodied would outlast everything visible, and promise, perhaps, survival. The Cro-Magnons lived with fear and amazement in a culture of Arrival, facing many mysteries. Their culture lasted for some 20,000 years. We live in a dominant culture of ceaseless Departure and Progress that has so far lasted two or three centuries. Today's culture, instead of facing mysteries, persistently tries to outflank them.　　—JOHN BERGER

The job of the artist is always to deepen the mystery.
　　—FRANCIS BACON

Beauty

When we contemplate the whole globe as one great dew-drop, striped and dotted with continents and islands, flying through space with other stars all singing and shining together as one, the whole universe appears as an infinite storm of beauty.　　　　　—JOHN MUIR

Isn't it enough to see that a garden is beautiful without having to believe that there are fairies at the bottom of it too?

　　　　　—DOUGLAS ADAMS, *The Ultimate Hitchhiker's*
Guide to the Galaxy

If you can't see anything beautiful about yourself get a better mirror.　　　　　—SHANE KOYCZAN, "To This Day"

If you retain nothing else, always remember the most important rule of beauty, which is: who cares?

　　　　　—TINA FEY

Why are numbers beautiful? It's like asking why is Beethoven's Ninth Symphony beautiful. If you don't see why, someone can't tell you. I know numbers are beautiful. If they aren't beautiful, nothing is.

—PAUL ERDŐS

The truth isn't always beauty, but the hunger for it is.

—NADINE GORDIMER

You Don't Have to Be Pretty. You don't owe prettiness to anyone. Not to your boyfriend/spouse/partner, not to your co-workers, especially not to random men on the street. You don't owe it to your mother, you don't owe it to your children, you don't owe it to civilization in general. Prettiness is not a rent you pay for occupying a space marked "female."

—ERIN MCKEAN

"What makes the desert beautiful," said the little prince, "is that somewhere it hides a well."

—ANTOINE DE SAINT-EXUPÉRY, *The Little Prince*

I believe in Michelangelo, Velasquez, and Rembrandt; in the might of design, the mystery of color, the redemption of all things by Beauty everlasting, and the message of Art that has made these hands blessed.
—GEORGE BERNARD SHAW, *The Doctor's Dilemma*

For me, the study of these laws is inseparable from a love of Nature in all its manifestations. The beauty of the basic laws of natural science, as revealed in the study of particles and of the cosmos, is allied to the litheness of a merganser diving in a pure Swedish lake, or the grace of a dolphin leaving shining trails at night in the Gulf of California. —MURRAY GELL-MANN

The most common error made in matters of appearance is the belief that one should let the true beauty of one's soul shine through. If there are places on your body where this is a possibility, you are not attractive—you are leaking. —FRAN LEBOWITZ

The most beautiful experience we can have is the mysterious. It is the fundamental emotion that stands at the cradle of true art and true science.
—ALBERT EINSTEIN

Belief

Ignorance is preferable to error, and he is less remote from the truth who believes nothing than he who believes what is wrong. —THOMAS JEFFERSON

It's hard to be religious when certain people are never incinerated by bolts of lightning.
—BILL WATTERSON, *Calvin and Hobbes*

A faith which cannot survive collision with the truth is not worth many regrets. —ARTHUR C. CLARKE

I contend we are both atheists, I just believe in one fewer god than you do. When you understand why you dismiss all the other possible gods, you will understand why I dismiss yours. —STEPHEN F. ROBERTS

Beliefs can be permanent, but beliefs can also be flexible. Personally, if I find out my belief is wrong, I change my mind. —LISA RANDALL

I believe in man . . . by "man" I mean man, woman and child. I believe that my duty to man is total service . . . outside man I owe none else any duties.

—Tai Solarin

Skepticism is my nature, Freethought is my methodology, Agnosticism is my conclusion, Atheism is my opinion and Humanitarianism is my motivation.

—Jerry W. DeWitt

Science adjusts its views based on what's observed. Faith is the denial of observation so that belief can be preserved.

—Tim Minchin, "Storm"

I believe in the indomitable human spirit and the amazing capacity we have for understanding the world; for love, joy and happiness. Science not only does not take away any of those things, it adds to the sum of human knowledge. —Michael Shermer

I do believe in the beauty and the awe-inspiring mystery of the science that's out there that we haven't discovered yet, that there are scientific explanations for phenomena that we call mystical because we don't know any better.

—Jodie Foster

What we think, or what we know, or what we believe is, in the end, of little consequence. The only consequence is what we do. —JOHN RUSKIN

I don't want you to follow me or anyone else . . . I would not lead you into the promised land if I could, because if I could lead you in, somebody else would lead you out.

—EUGENE V. DEBS

You can never have too much butter—that is my belief. If I have a religion, that's it. —NORA EPHRON

When I told the people of Northern Ireland that I was an atheist, a woman in the audience stood up and said, "Yes, but is it the God of the Catholics or the God of the Protestants in whom you don't believe?"

—QUENTIN CRISP

Independence is my happiness, and I view things as they are, without regard to place or person; my country is the world, and my religion is to do good. —THOMAS PAINE

We despise all reverences and all the objects of reverence which are outside the pale of our own list of sacred things. And yet, with strange inconsistency, we are shocked when other people despise and defile the things which are holy to us. —MARK TWAIN

If you've got a religious belief that withers in the face of observations of the natural world, you ought to rethink your beliefs—rethinking the world isn't an option.
—PZ MYERS

If there's something you really want to believe, that's what you should question the most. —PENN JILLETTE

Because here's something else that's weird but true: in the day-to day trenches of adult life, there is actually no such thing as atheism. There is no such thing as not wor-shipping. Everybody worships. The only choice we get is what to worship. —DAVID FOSTER WALLACE

Sacred cows make the tastiest hamburger.
—ABBIE HOFFMAN

I know that in environments of uncertainty, fear, and hunger, the human being is dwarfed and shaped without his being aware of it, just as the plant struggling under a stone does not know its own condition. Only when the stone is removed can it spring up freely into the light. But the power to spring up is inherent, and only death

puts an end to it. I feel no need for any other faith than
my faith in human beings.   —PEARL S. BUCK

A man's got to believe something, and I believe I'll have
another drink.   —PETER DE VRIES, *The Vale of Laughter*

When one longs for a drink, it seems as though one could
drink a whole ocean—that is faith; but when one begins
to drink, one can only drink altogether two glasses—that
is science.   —ANTON CHEKHOV

Show Me Before I Believe is my motto.
                                        —ALFRED T. KISUBI

There's nothing that can help you explain your own beliefs better than trying to explain them to an inquisitive
child.   —FRANK CLARK

An idea isn't responsible for the people who believe in it.
                                  —DON MARQUIS (attributed)

I do not believe in Belief. But this is an Age of Faith, and
there are so many militant creeds that, in self defense, one
has to formulate a creed of one's own. . . . Tolerance,
good temper and sympathy—they are what matter really, and if the human race is not to collapse they must
come to the front before long.   —E. M. FORSTER

When you hear for the first time the music you have composed, there is that astonishing moment when the idea that you carried in your heart and your mind comes back to you in the hands of a musician. . . . The experience of that is my god.   —PHILIP GLASS

I never believed in Santa Claus because I knew no white dude would come into my neighborhood after dark.
          —DICK GREGORY

For some time I was saying, "God is Truth," but that did not satisfy me. So now I say, "Truth is God." . . . Do you think I am superstitious? I am super-atheist.
          —MOHANDAS K. GANDHI

What do I believe in? I believe in sun. In rock. In the dogma of the sun and the doctrine of the rock. I believe in blood, fire, woman, rivers, eagles, storm, drums, flutes, banjos, and broom-tailed horses.
          —EDWARD ABBEY

The foolish reject what they see and not what they think; the wise reject what they think and not what they see.
          —HUANG PO

The world would be astonished if it knew how great a proportion of its brightest ornaments—of those most distinguished even in popular estimation for wisdom and virtue—are complete skeptics in religion.
          —JOHN STUART MILL

> My Imagination is a Monastery
> and I am its Monk.
>
> —JOHN KEATS

I am an individual and a believer in liberty. That is all the politics I have. I don't want to create a revolution—I just want to create a few more films.

—CHARLIE CHAPLIN

It isn't necessary to have something to believe in. It's only necessary to believe that somewhere there's something worthy of belief.

—ALFRED BESTER, *The Stars My Destination*

Until the Greeks filled libraries with skepticism and secularism, no one ever thought of having a religion where the central active gesture was to believe.

—JENNIFER MICHAEL HECHT

An Atheist loves his fellow man instead of god. An Atheist believes that heaven is something for which we should work now—here on earth for all men together to enjoy. . . . He wants disease conquered, poverty vanished, war eliminated.   —MADALYN MURRAY O'HAIR

My theology, briefly, is that the universe was dictated, but not signed.

—CHRISTOPHER MORLEY, "Safe and Sane"

When confronted with anyone who holds my lack of religious faith in such contempt, I say, "It's the way God made me." —RICKY GERVAIS

I have made a great discovery. I no longer believe in anything. Objects don't exist for me except insofar as a rapport exists between them or between them and myself. When one attains this harmony, one reaches a sort of intellectual nonexistence—what I can only describe as a sense of peace—which makes everything possible and right. Life then becomes perpetual revelation.   —GEORGES BRAQUE

From the point of view of a tapeworm, man was created by God to serve the appetite of the tapeworm.

—EDWARD ABBEY

The eyes are the windows to where the soul is supposed to be.   —TINA FEY

I am a lover of truth, a worshipper of freedom, a celebrant at the altar of language and purity and tolerance. That is my religion, and every day I am sorely, grossly, heinously and deeply offended, wounded, mortified and injured by a thousand different blasphemies against it. —STEPHEN FRY

Jesus Christ is the only God. And so am I. And so are you.
—WILLIAM BLAKE

For people of faith, I think the greatest compliment I could pay them is to respect their genuinely held beliefs and not to engage in some pretence about mine.
—AUSTRALIAN PRIME MINISTER JULIA GILLARD

It often occurs to me that if, against all odds, there is a judgmental God and heaven, it will come to pass that when the pearly gates open, those who had the valor to think for themselves will be escorted to the head of the line, garlanded, and given their own personal audience.
—E. O. WILSON

The idea of the sacred is quite simply one of the most conservative notions in any culture, because it seeks to turn other ideas—uncertainty, progress, change—into crimes.
—SALMAN RUSHDIE

Atheists don't use their dying to bargain for a better seat at the table; indeed they may not even believe supper is being served. They are not storing up "merit." They just smile because their heart is ripe. They are kind for no particular reason; they just love.
—STEPHEN LEVINE

I believe there's nothing we can know except that we should be kind to each other and do what we can for people.

—KATHARINE HEPBURN

To find the divine and the helpful in the mean and familiar, to find religion without the aid of any supernatural machinery, to see the spiritual, the eternal life in and through the life that now is—in short, to see the rude, prosy earth as a star in the heavens, like the rest, is indeed the lesson of all others the hardest to learn.

—JOHN BURROUGHS

Atheism in its negation of gods is at the same time the strongest affirmation of man, and through man, the eternal yea to life, purpose, and beauty.

—EMMA GOLDMAN

If I go to a play I do not enjoy it less because I do not believe that it is divinely created and divinely conducted, that it will last forever instead of stopping at eleven, that many details of it will remain in my memory after a few months, or that it will have any particular moral effect upon me. And I enjoy life as I enjoy that play.

—SINCLAIR LEWIS

The great civilizer on earth seems to have been doubt. Doubt, the constantly debated and flexible inner condition of theological uncertainty, seems to have held people in thrall to ethical behavior, while the true believers of whatever stamp, religious or religious-statist, have done the murdering. —E. L. DOCTOROW

They say the streets are going to be beautiful in Heaven. Well, I'm trying to make the streets beautiful here. . . . When it's clean and beautiful, I think America is heaven. And some people are hell.

—BUTTERFLY MCQUEEN

That's atheism—just doing the intellectual work of explaining and debating things without reference to the supernatural—not devising ever-more-intricate proofs that there is no God. —MATTHEW YGLESIAS

I don't believe in God. I believe in Al Pacino.

—JAVIER BARDEM

The only atheist is someone who does not make a God even out of atheism itself. —GABRIEL LAUBER

It does not matter whether God exists. Any good that God is able or willing to do is insignificant compared to what we human beings must do for ourselves.

—NORM R. ALLEN, JR.

I wish there was a place where atheists could all get together and sing songs about physics. I love being a rationalist but it's lonely.   —SIMON PEGG

If the concept of God has any validity or use, it can only be to make us larger, freer, and more loving. If God cannot do this, then it is time we got rid of Him.

—JAMES BALDWIN

Heaven, such as it is, is right here on earth. Behold: my revelation: I stand at the door in the morning, and lo, there is a newspaper, in sight like unto an emerald. And holy, holy, holy is the coffee, which was, and is, and is to come. And hark, I hear the voice of an angel round about the radio saying, "Since my baby left me I found a new place to dwell." And lo, after this I beheld a great multitude, which no man could number, of shoes. And after these things I will hasten unto a taxicab and to a theater, where a ticket will be given unto me, and lo, it will be a matinee, and a film that doeth great wonders. And when it is finished, the heavens will open, and out will cometh a rain fragrant as myrrh, and yea, I have an umbrella.   —SARAH VOWELL

Doubt grows with knowledge.

—JOHANN WOLFGANG VON GOETHE

Like many people, I have no religion, and I am just sitting in a small boat drifting with the tide. I live in the doubts of my duty. . . . I think there is dignity in this, just to go on working. —FEDERICO FELLINI

For those who believe in God, most of the big questions are answered. But for those of us who can't readily accept the God formula, the big answers don't remain stonewritten. We adjust to new conditions and discoveries. We are pliable. Love need not be a command or faith a dictum. I am my own God. We are here to unlearn the teachings of the church, state and our educational system. We are here to drink beer. We are here to kill war. We are here to laugh at the odds and live our lives so well that Death will tremble to take us. —CHARLES BUKOWSKI

If God dwells inside us like some people say, I sure hope He likes enchiladas, because that's what He's getting.
—JACK HANDEY

Sometimes a concept is baffling not because it is profound but because it is wrong. —E. O. WILSON

Perhaps I am just a hopeless rationalist, but isn't fascination as comforting as solace? Isn't nature immeasurably more interesting for its complexities and its lack of conformity to our hopes? Isn't curiosity as wondrously and fundamentally human as compassion?

—STEPHEN JAY GOULD

Believe those who are seeking the truth; doubt those who find it. —ANDRÉ GIDE

I believe that anything worth its salt in the arts must create a wobble. We are not polestars. We are here struggling in the dynamics of justice, between the absolutism of faith and reasonable doubt. That's what I want my work to do. —VAN DYKE PARKS

Without doubts, without a standpoint reached through questioning, human beings can't acquire knowledge.

—AYAAN HIRSI ALI

People search for certainty. But there is no certainty. People are terrified—how can you live and not know? It is not odd at all. You only think you know, as a matter of fact. And most of your actions are based on incomplete knowledge and you really don't know what it is all about, or what the purpose of the world is, or know a great deal of other things. It is possible to live and not know. —RICHARD P. FEYNMAN

The outcome of any serious research can only be to make two questions grow where only one grew before.

—THORSTEIN VEBLEN

It is not the answer that enlightens, but the question.

—EUGENE IONESCO

The only thing that makes life possible is permanent, intolerable uncertainty: not knowing what comes next.

—URSULA K. LE GUIN, *The Left Hand of Darkness*

All gods *were* immortal.

—STANISLAW J. LEC

I have never made but one prayer to God, a very short one: "O Lord, make my enemies ridiculous." And God granted it.

—VOLTAIRE

About the gods I have no means of knowing either that they exist or that they do not exist or what they are to look at. Many things prevent my knowing. Among others, the fact that they are never seen.

—PROTAGORAS

I think we're capable of extraordinary things, human beings. I call that God-like.

—STUDS TERKEL

I'm not normally a praying man, but if you're up there, please save me, Superman.

—HOMER SIMPSON

Impiety: your irreverence toward my deity.

—AMBROSE BIERCE

Men tend to have the beliefs that suit their passions. Cruel men believe in a cruel God, and use their belief to excuse their cruelty. Only kindly men believe in a kindly God, and they would be kindly in any case.

—BERTRAND RUSSELL

Of all the animosities which have existed among mankind, those which are caused by difference of sentiment in religion appear to be the most inveterate and distressing, and ought most to be deprecated.

—GEORGE WASHINGTON

I read about an Eskimo hunter who asked the local missionary priest, "If I did not know about God and sin, would I go to hell?" "No," said the priest, "not if you did not know." "Then why," asked the Eskimo earnestly, "did you tell me?"

—ANNIE DILLARD

Chance and Coincidence

The essence of life is statistical improbability on a colossal scale.
—RICHARD DAWKINS

The man who is not dead still has a chance.
—LEBANESE PROVERB

We are here because one odd group of fishes had a peculiar fin anatomy that could transform into legs for terrestrial creatures; because the earth never froze entirely during an ice age; because a small and tenuous species, arising in Africa a quarter of a million years ago, has managed, so far, to survive by hook and by crook. We may yearn for a "higher" answer—but none exists. This explanation, though superficially troubling, if not terrifying, is ultimately liberating and exhilarating. We cannot read the meaning of life passively in the facts of nature. We must construct these answers ourselves—from our own wisdom and ethical sense. There is no other way.
—STEPHEN JAY GOULD

Of course I don't believe in it. But I understand that it's lucky whether you believe in it or not.

—NIELS BOHR, on hanging a horseshoe on his wall

A pinch of probably is worth a pound of perhaps.

—JAMES THURBER

You never know what worse luck your bad luck has saved you from.

—CORMAC MCCARTHY, *No Country for Old Men*

Most of the species that have ever existed are now extinct. Extinction is the rule. Survival is the exception.

—CARL SAGAN

It is known that Whistler when asked how long it took him to paint one of his "nocturnes" answered: "All of my life." With the same rigor he could have said that all of the centuries that preceded the moment when he painted were necessary. From that correct application of the law of causality it follows that the slightest event presupposes the inconceivable universe and, conversely, that the universe needs even the slightest of events.   —JORGE LUIS BORGES

Statistically, the probability of any one of us being here is so small that you'd think the mere fact of existing would keep us all in a contented dazzlement of surprise.

—LEWIS THOMAS

Depend on the rabbit's foot if you will, but remember: it didn't work for the rabbit.

—R. E. SHAY

Change

All flows, nothing stays.   —HERACLITUS

If the shoe doesn't fit, must we change the foot?
                                              —GLORIA STEINEM

Our condition is the condition of all things. The universe exists forever, but all within it changes. The everlasting universe is composed of the endless birth and passing of all its forms. The universe exists within the passing of its creatures.   —KENNETH L. PATTON

Very early, I knew that the only object in life was to grow.   —MARGARET FULLER

Only the ephemeral is of lasting value.
                                              —EUGENE IONESCO

Every generation laughs at the old fashions, but follows religiously the new.   —HENRY DAVID THOREAU

It is said an Eastern monarch once charged his wise men to invent him a sentence to be ever in view, and which should be true and appropriate in all times and situations. They presented him the words: "And this, too, shall pass away." How much it expresses! How chastening in the hour of pride! How consoling in the depths of affliction!

—ABRAHAM LINCOLN

We need not destroy the past. It is gone.

—JOHN CAGE

You can recognize a pioneer by the arrows in his back.

—BEVERLY RUBIK

If you want to make enemies, try to change something.

—WOODROW WILSON

If you don't become the ocean you'll be seasick every day.

—LEONARD COHEN, "Good Advice for Someone Like Me"

Of all existing things some are in our power, and others are not in our power.

—EPICTETUS

But I know also, that laws and institutions must go hand in hand with the progress of the human mind. As that becomes more developed, more enlightened, as new discoveries are made, new truths disclosed, and manners and opinions change with the change of circumstances, institutions must advance also, and keep pace with the times. —THOMAS JEFFERSON

You may not be able to change the world, but at least you can embarrass the guilty. —JESSICA MITFORD

It is not by sitting still at a grand distance, and calling the human race *larvae*, that men are to be helped . . . but by doing unweariedly the particular work we were born to do. —RALPH WALDO EMERSON

Here's what we can do to change the world, right now, to a better ride. Take all that money we spend on weapons and defenses each year and instead spend it feeding and clothing and educating the poor of the world, which it would pay for many times over, not one human being excluded, and we could explore space, together, both inner and outer, forever, in peace. —BILL HICKS

Of course, in the long run, the great trivial purpose of maximum entropy will appear to be the most enduring of all. —NORBERT WIENER

Rust never sleeps. —NEIL YOUNG

Death

I believe that the purpose of death is the release of love.
—LAURIE ANDERSON

Nothing lasts but nothing is lost.
—TERENCE MCKENNA

When everyone in the world admits they're going to die we'll really start getting some stuff done.
—CAITLIN MORAN

Don't waste any time mourning. Organize!
—JOE HILL

What gives dignity to death is the dignity of the life that preceded it.   —SHERWIN B. NULAND

It feels to me that the process of dying is actually dying into a greater presence. It isn't lessening, it's actually more. And we die into greater awe, greater splendor, greater terror, and greater presence.   —LI-YOUNG LEE

Millions long for immortality who don't know what to do with themselves on a rainy Sunday afternoon.
—SUSAN ERTZ, *Anger in the Sky*

Death is nothing so long as one can survive through one's children.   —RWANDAN PROVERB

It's funny the way most people love the dead. You have to die before they think you are worth anything. Once you are dead, you are made for life. When I die, just keep on playing the records.   —JIMI HENDRIX

Nature (meaning Death) always wins but that doesn't mean we have to bow and grovel to it.
—DONNA TARTT, *The Goldfinch*

Put song and music before you / Cast all evil behind you / Think of your joys / Until that day has come of landing / At the land that loves silence.
—"The Harper's Song," inscribed in the Tomb of Neferhotep ca. 1300 BCE

There are three deaths. The first is when the body ceases to function. The second is when the body is consigned to the grave. The third is that moment, sometime in the future, when your name is spoken for the last time.

—DAVID EAGLEMAN, "Metamorphosis"

There are many things in this world that are an outrage, to be sure, but death at our current life expectancy doesn't strike me as one of them.   —DAVID RAKOFF

Even if it means oblivion, friends, I'll welcome it, because it won't be nothing. We'll be alive again in a thousand blades of grass, and a million leaves; we'll be falling in the raindrops and blowing in the fresh breeze; we'll be glittering in the dew under the stars and the moon out there in the physical world, which is our true home and always was.   —PHILIP PULLMAN, *The Amber Spyglass*

To live till you die is to live long enough.

—LAO TZU

Life on Earth is 3.8 billion years old and it has not stopped reproducing since it started. You may disappear but you may also become part of a new form—not a ghost, but a grandchild.   —DORION SAGAN

I hope that after I die, people will say of me: "That guy sure owed me a lot of money."   —JACK HANDEY

Death will be a great relief. No more interviews.

—KATHARINE HEPBURN

To aspire to be superhuman is a most discreditable admission that you lack the guts, the wit, the moderating judgment to be successfully and consummately human.

—ALDOUS HUXLEY

What is terrible is not death but the lives people live or don't live up until their death.

—CHARLES BUKOWSKI

Jerónimo, my grandfather, swineherd and story-teller, feeling death about to arrive and take him, went and said goodbye to the trees in the yard, one by one, embracing them and crying because he knew he wouldn't see them again.

—JOSÉ SARAMAGO

There is no reason for amazement: surely one always knew that cultures decay, and life's end is death.

—ROBINSON JEFFERS, "The Purse-Seine"

Who knows but life be that which men call death, And death what men call life?

—EURIPIDES

People living deeply have no fear of death.

—ANAÏS NIN

Death is certain, replacing both the siren-song of Paradise and the dread of Hell. Life on this earth, with all its mystery and beauty and pain, is then to be lived far more intensely: we stumble and get up, we are sad, confident, insecure, feel loneliness and joy and love. There is nothing more; but I want nothing more.

—AYAAN HIRSI ALI

Life is a great surprise. I do not see why death should not be an even greater one.

—VLADIMIR NABOKOV, *Pale Fire*

Those who die leave as many biographies as there are people who knew them. —KENNETH L. PATTON

All say: "How hard it is that we have to die"—a strange complaint to come from the mouths of people who have had to live.

—MARK TWAIN, *The Tragedy of Pudd'nhead Wilson*

Death is the dark backing a mirror needs if we are to see anything.

—SAUL BELLOW, *Humboldt's Gift*

Perhaps the whole root of our trouble, the human trouble, is that we will sacrifice all the beauty of our lives, will imprison ourselves in totems, taboos, crosses, blood sacrifices, steeples, mosques, races, armies, flags, nations, in order to deny the fact of death, which is the only fact we have.   —JAMES BALDWIN

I would rather be ashes than dust! I would rather that my spark should burn out in a brilliant blaze than it should be stifled by dry-rot. I would rather be a superb meteor, every atom of me in magnificent glow, than a sleepy and permanent planet. The proper function of man is to live, not to exist. I shall not waste my days in trying to prolong them. I shall use my time.

—JACK LONDON

I have little confidence in any enterprise or business or investment that promises dividends only after the death of the stockholders.   —ROBERT G. INGERSOLL

Death . . . the most awful of evils, is nothing to us, seeing that, when we are, death is not come, and when death is come, we are not.   —EPICURUS

It was happening all the time, unnoticed, and it was the thing that really mattered. What really mattered in life, what gave it weight, was death.

—JEFFREY EUGENIDES, *Middlesex*

Death must be so beautiful. To lie in the soft brown earth, with the grasses waving above one's head, and listen to silence. To have no yesterday, and no tomorrow. To forget time, to forgive life, to be at peace.

—OSCAR WILDE, "The Canterville Ghost"

Only when you accept that one day you'll die can you let go, and make the best out of life. And that's the big secret. That's the miracle.   —GABRIEL BÁ, *Daytripper*

It's quite possible in 200 years' time people will look back and the only thing people will remember about us is that we listened to the Beatles.   —ANTHONY LANE

We will sing to you, Doctor. The universe will sing you to your sleep. This song is ending. But the story never ends.

—OOD SIGMA, to the Tenth incarnation of the Doctor, in *Doctor Who*

I know that nothing is destructible; things merely change forms. When the consciousness we know as life ceases, I know that I shall still be part and parcel of the world. I was a part before the sun rolled into shape and burst forth in the glory of change. I was, when the earth was hurled out from its fiery rim. I shall return with the earth to Father Sun, and still exist in substance when the

sun has lost its fire, and disintegrated into infinity to perhaps become a part of the whirling rubble of space.

—ZORA NEALE HURSTON

Something about the meaning of life changes when you
realize deeply that it won't last forever . . . we bring a
deeper commitment to our happiness when we fully understand . . . that our time left is limited and we really
need to make it count. —ELISABETH KÜBLER-ROSS

He wanted his body transported in the bed of a pickup
truck. He wanted to be buried as soon as possible. He
wanted no undertakers. No embalming, for God sake!
No coffin. Just an old sleeping bag. ". . . Disregard all
state laws concerning burial. I want my body to help fer-
tilize the growth of a cactus or cliff rose or sagebrush or
tree."

—DOUG PEACOCK, on Edward Abbey's
wishes for his funeral

Those who so greatly exalt incorruptibility, inalterabil-
ity, etc. are reduced to talking this way, I believe, by their
great desire to go on living, and by the terror they have
of death. They do not reflect that if men were immortal,
they themselves would never have come into the world.

—GALILEO GALILEI

My whole religion is this: do every duty, and expect no reward for it, either here or hereafter.

—BERTRAND RUSSELL, at age sixteen

I think from my experience in war and life and science, it all has made me believe that we have one life on this planet. We have one chance to live it and to contribute to the future of society and the future of life. The only "afterlife" is what other people remember of you.

—CRAIG VENTER

When I die I shall be content to vanish into nothingness. No show, however good, could conceivably be good for ever.

—H. L. MENCKEN

The history of a species, or any natural phenomenon that requires unbroken continuity in a world of trouble, works like a batting streak. . . . The gambler must eventually go bust. His aim can only be to stick around as long as possible, to have some fun while he's at it, and, if he happens to be a moral agent as well, to worry about staying the course with honor.

—STEPHEN JAY GOULD

That it will never come again / Is what makes life so sweet.

—EMILY DICKINSON, Poem #1741

[The fact that I'm going to die soon] bugs me sometimes too. But not so much as you think. . . . When you get as old as I am, you start to realize that you've told most of the good stuff you know to other people anyway.

—RICHARD P. FEYNMAN

Type faster.

—ISAAC ASIMOV, on being asked by Barbara Walters what he would do if told he had only six months to live

I never saw one of my peasant neighbors cogitating over the countenance and assurance with which he would pass this last hour. Nature teaches him not to think about death except when he is dying. And then he has better grace about it than Aristotle, whom death oppresses doubly, by itself and by a long foreknowledge.

—MONTAIGNE

The best break anybody ever gets is in bein' alive in the first place. An' you don't unnerstan' what a perfect deal it is until you realizes that you ain't gone be stuck with it forever, either. —WALT KELLY, *Pogo*

I have no idea what's awaiting me, or what will happen when this all ends. For the moment I know this: there are sick people and they need curing.

—ALBERT CAMUS, *The Plague*

We must be born with an intuition of mortality. Before we know the word for it, before we know that there are words, out we come, bloodied and squalling . . . with the knowledge that for all the points of the compass, there's only one direction and time is its only measure.

—TOM STOPPARD, *Rosencrantz and Guildenstern Are Dead*

I know why we try to keep the dead alive: we try to keep them alive in order to keep them with us. I also know that if we are to live ourselves there comes a point at which we must relinquish the dead, let them go, keep them dead. —JOAN DIDION

If you were going to die soon and had only one phone call you could make who would you call and what would you say? And why are you waiting?

—STEPHEN LEVINE

Emotions

Let everything happen to you: beauty and terror. / Just keep going. No feeling is final.

—RAINER MARIA RILKE,
"Go to the Limits of Your Longing"

Let us not look back in anger or forward in fear, but around in awareness. —JAMES THURBER

This machine surrounds hate and forces it to surrender.
—Inscription on Pete Seeger's banjo

In other words, we think we have found the basic copying mechanisms by which life comes from life. . . . You can understand that we are very excited.

—FRANCIS CRICK, explaining his discovery of
the DNA double helix in a letter to his son

A poor person who is unhappy is in a better position than a rich person who is unhappy, because the poor person has hope. He thinks money would help.

—JEAN KERR

There is but one coward on earth, and that is the coward that dare not know. —W. E. B. DU BOIS

Grab the broom of anger and drive off the beast of fear.

—ZORA NEALE HURSTON

Our dreams, our impulses, our appetites, our drives, our desires, are not things to apologize for.

—STEPHEN FRY

That the situation is hopeless should not prevent us from doing our best. —ALDO LEOPOLD

Hatred, which could destroy so much, never failed to destroy the man who hated and this was an immutable law. —JAMES BALDWIN

A wet man does not fear rain. —RUSSIAN PROVERB

All they know of hate is that it couldn't beat the love out of me. —ANDREA GIBSON, "Ashes"

You can discover what your enemy fears most by observing the means he uses to frighten you.

—ERIC HOFFER

Nor is the outlook of unbelief, to my way of thinking, a bleak one. It is merely rooted in courage and not in fear.

—CARL VAN DOREN

It is a fine thing to face machine guns for immortality and a medal, but isn't it a fine thing, too, to face calumny, injustice and loneliness for the truth which makes men free?

—H. L. MENCKEN

Nothing in life is to be feared. It is only to be understood. Now is the time to understand more, so that we may fear less.

—MARIE CURIE

Hope is the feeling we have that the feeling we have is not permanent.

—MIGNON MCLAUGHLIN

However vast the darkness, we must supply our own light.

—STANLEY KUBRICK

Man can do what he wants, but he cannot want what he
wants.   —ARTHUR SCHOPENHAUER

I know what "nothing" means, and keep on playing.
                              —JOAN DIDION, *Play It as It Lays*

Incessant potential catastrophe is the human condition,
is in fact the price of possessing consciousness, and I am
determined to live with greater ease from now on, and
not to let anyone scare me about the future, because the
truth is, the worst thing that could ever happen to you is
death, and that's going to happen despite all your worry
and effort, so it's simply irrational not to say fuck it.
                              —JOHN JEREMIAH SULLIVAN

Everything can be taken from a man but one thing: the
last of the human freedoms—to choose one's attitude in
any given set of circumstances, to choose one's own way.
                              —VIKTOR FRANKL

Hope is like a road in the country; there was never a
road, but when many people walk on it, the road comes
into existence.   —LIN YUTANG

Fear builds its phantoms which are more fearsome than
reality itself, and reality when calmly analyzed and its
consequences willingly accepted loses much of its terror.
                              —JAWAHARLAL NEHRU

A hero is someone who does what he can.
—ROMAIN ROLLAND, *Jean-Christophe*

Childbirth is more admirable than conquest, more amazing than self-defense, and as courageous as either one.
—GLORIA STEINEM

I have loved the stars too fondly to be fearful of the night.
—SARAH WILLIAMS, "The Old Astronomer"

Why hate someone for the color of their skin when there are much better reasons to hate them?
—DENIS LEARY (attributed)

A lot of what looks like a lack of willpower is, from another perspective, a series of positive choices in favor of one of the other kinds of happiness.
—JENNIFER MICHAEL HECHT

Question with boldness even the existence of a god; because, if there be one, he must more approve the homage of reason, than that of blindfolded fear.
—THOMAS JEFFERSON

I've never met a healthy person who worried much about his health or a good person who worried much about his soul.
—J. B. S. HALDANE

The most anxious man in a prison is the governor.

—GEORGE BERNARD SHAW

Whate'er's begun in anger ends in shame.

—BENJAMIN FRANKLIN

I have great faith in optimism as a guiding principle, if only because it offers us the opportunity of creating a self-fulfilling prophecy. —ARTHUR C. CLARKE

Take care not to make your pain greater by your complaints. —SENECA

In the depth of winter, I finally learned that within me there lay an invincible summer. —ALBERT CAMUS

We tell lies when we are afraid . . . afraid of what we don't know, afraid of what others will think, afraid of what will be found out about us. But every time we tell a lie, the thing that we fear grows stronger.

—TAD WILLIAMS, *To Green Angel Tower*

Needless fear and panic over disease and misfortune that seldom materialize are simply bad habits. By proper ventilation and illumination of the mind it is possible to cultivate tolerance, poise and real courage.

—ÉLIE METCHNIKOFF

It is hope that gives life a meaning. And hope is based on the prospect of being able one day to turn the actual world into a possible one that looks better.

—FRANÇOIS JACOB

And the only thing people regret is that they didn't live boldly enough, that they didn't invest enough heart, didn't love enough. Nothing else really counts at all.

—TED HUGHES

For as children tremble and fear everything in the blind darkness, so we in the light sometimes fear what is no more to be feared than the things children in the dark hold in terror and imagine will come true. This terror therefore and darkness of mind must be dispelled not by the rays of the sun and glittering shafts of day, but by the aspect and law of nature.

—LUCRETIUS

Although the world is full of suffering, it is full also of the overcoming of it.

—HELEN KELLER

I've never really thought of myself as depressed as much as paralyzed by hope.

—MARIA BAMFORD

There's something just as inevitable as death. And that's life. Life, life, life! Think of the power of the universe—turning the Earth, growing the trees. That's the same

power within you—if you'll only have the courage and
the will to use it.   —CHARLIE CHAPLIN, *Limelight*

At least half of my songs deal with ambivalence, feeling
two things at once. . . . I prefer neurotic people. I like to
hear rumblings beneath the surface.

        —STEPHEN SONDHEIM

I never saw a discontented tree.   —JOHN MUIR

"I'm bored" is a useless thing to say. I mean, you live in
a great, big, vast world that you've seen none percent of.
Even the inside of your own mind is endless, it goes on
forever, inwardly, do you understand? The fact that
you're alive is amazing, so you don't get to say "I'm
bored."   —LOUIS C. K.

Western civilization places so much emphasis on the
idea of hope that we sacrifice the present moment.
Hope is for the future. It cannot help us discover joy,
peace, or enlightenment in the present moment. Many
religions are based on the notion of hope, and this
teaching about refraining from hope may create a
strong reaction. But the shock can bring about something important. I do not mean that you should not
have hope, but that hope is not enough. . . . Peace
work is not a means. Each step we make should be

peace. . . . We don't need the future. We can smile and relax. Everything we want is right here in the present moment. —THICH NHAT HANH

My only regret is that I have not drunk more champagne in my life.

—JOHN MAYNARD KEYNES

Freedom

Man is free at the instant he wants to be.
—Voltaire, *Brutus*

Every little increase in human freedom has been fought over ferociously between those who want us to know more and be wiser and stronger, and those who want us to obey and be humble and submit.
—Philip Pullman, *The Subtle Knife*

The function of freedom is to free someone else.
—Toni Morrison

If liberty means anything at all, it means the right to tell people what they do not want to hear.
—George Orwell

The only man who is really free is the one who can turn down an invitation to dinner without giving any excuse.
—Jules Renard (attributed)

Freedom is available, the trick is to stop looking out there for it and to sit down, shut up, and see for yourself that your truest nature, however deeply buried or obscured, is closer to love than anything else.

—NOAH LEVINE

I contemplate with sovereign reverence that act of the whole American people which declared that their legislature should make no law respecting an establishment of religion, or prohibit the free exercise thereof, thus building a wall of separation between church and state.

—THOMAS JEFFERSON

The cost of liberty is less than the price of repression.

—W. E. B. DU BOIS

In fact, the real disturbers of the peace are those who, in a free state, seek to curtail the liberty of judgment which they are unable to tyrannize over.

—BARUCH SPINOZA

You measure democracy by the freedom it gives its dissidents, not the freedom it gives its assimilated conformists.

—ABBIE HOFFMAN

Free speech is the bedrock of liberty and a free society. And yes, it includes the right to blaspheme and offend.

—AYAAN HIRSI ALI

Burn all the maps / to your body

—RICHARD BRAUTIGAN,
"The Double-Bed Dream Gallows"

What part of "liberation for women" is not for you? Is it freedom to vote? The right not to be owned by the man you marry? The campaign for equal pay? "Vogue," by Madonna? Jeans? Did all that good shit GET ON YOUR NERVES? Or were you just DRUNK AT THE TIME OF SURVEY? —CAITLIN MORAN

Everybody says that they have better things to do, but teenagers are the only ones who really do have better things to do. When I meet a teenager, I think, *They could be getting high in a car.* —DAVID SEDARIS

There is no safety in numbers, or in anything else.
—JAMES THURBER

Freedom is something that dies unless it's used.
—HUNTER S. THOMPSON

"But," you will say, "I feel free." This is an illusion, which may be compared to that of the fly in the fable, who, upon the pole of a heavy carriage, applauded himself for directing it. Man, who thinks himself free, is a fly, who imagines he has power to move the universe, while he is himself unknowingly carried along by it.

—BARON D'HOLBACH

Freedom is that space in which contradiction can reign; it is a never-ending debate. It is not in itself the answer to the question of morals but the conversation about that question.　　　　—SALMAN RUSHDIE

A pedestal is as much a prison as any small, confined space.　　　　—GLORIA STEINEM

I remember waking up one day with an epiphanous revelation: I am not a neo-Darwinist! It recalled an earlier experience, when I realized that I wasn't a humanistic Jew ... it was a simple declaration of independence from the surrounding group—the realization that there was a great freedom to be gained not from belonging, but from not belonging.　　　　—LYNN MARGULIS

The most important thing to do in your life is to not interfere with somebody else's life.　　　　—FRANK ZAPPA

Gratitude

The Universe is in a constant state of becoming—an ongoing miraculous creation. And every day we awaken to that miracle with gratitude, respect and compassion for all who share the gift of Being. —HAROLD RAMIS

We learned a lot about the Moon, but what we really learned was about the Earth. The fact that just from the distance of the Moon you can put your thumb up and you can hide the Earth behind your thumb. Everything that you've ever known, your loved ones, your business, the problems of the Earth itself—all behind your thumb. And how insignificant we really all are, but then how fortunate we are to have this body and to be able to enjoy living here amongst the beauty of the Earth itself.
                              —JIM LOVELL, Apollo astronaut

I'm not extravagant, I was brought up in the war. But I love the feeling that, if I wanted, I could buy a really expensive coat. The freedom that I could is enough.
                              —MARGARET DRABBLE

I don't believe in God, but I have this idea that if there were a God, or destiny of some kind looking down on us, that if he saw you taking anything for granted, he'd take it away. —HUGH LAURIE

When eating a fruit, think of the person who planted the tree. —VIETNAMESE PROVERB

Happiness

> I'm not guilty about pleasure.
>
> —JOHN WATERS

Happiness isn't on the road to anything. . . . Happiness is the road.

> —BOB DYLAN, quoting his grandmother,
> LYBBA KIRGHIZ EDELSTEIN

I got the blues thinking of the future, so I left off and made some marmalade. It's amazing how it cheers one up to shred oranges and scrub the floor.

> —D. H. LAWRENCE

The happy do not believe in miracles.

> —JOHANN WOLFGANG VON GOETHE,
> *Hermann and Dorothea*

One of the secrets of a happy life is continuous small treats.   —IRIS MURDOCH, *The Sea, The Sea*

Heaven is home. Utopia is here. Nirvana is now.
—EDWARD ABBEY

If you plan on being anything less than you are capable of being, you will probably be unhappy all the days of your life. —ABRAHAM MASLOW

Well, I'd rather be unhappy than have the sort of false, lying happiness you were having here.
—ALDOUS HUXLEY, *Brave New World*

"The best thing for being sad," replied Merlin, beginning to puff and blow, "is to learn something. That's the only thing that never fails. You may grow old and trembling in your anatomies, you may lie awake at night listening to the disorder of your veins, you may miss your only love, you may see the world about you devastated by evil lunatics, or know your honour trampled in the sewers of baser minds. There is only one thing for it then—to learn. Learn why the world wags and what wags it. That is the only thing which the mind can never exhaust, never alienate, never be tortured by, never fear or distrust, and never dream of regretting. Learning is the only thing for you. Look what a lot of things there are to learn."   —T. H. WHITE, *The Once and Future King*

I'm content. I like content better than happy, for sure. . . . Happy means you'll come down soon.
—ROSEANNE BARR

Grab every scrap of happiness while you can.
                          —Noel Coward, *Noel and Gertie*

There are shortcuts to happiness, and dancing is one of them.   —Vicki Baum

I have never been one of those who cares about happiness. Happiness is a strange notion. I am just not made for it. It has never been a goal of mine; I do not think in those terms.   —Werner Herzog

The only possible good in the universe is happiness. The time to be happy is now. The place to be happy is here. The way to be happy is to try to make others so.
                          —Robert G. Ingersoll

It is impossible to live a pleasant life without living wisely and well and justly, and it is impossible to live wisely and well and justly without living pleasantly.
                          —Epicurus

To me, the raveled sleeve of care is never more painlessly knitted up than in an evening alone in a chair snug yet copious, with a good light and an easily held little volume sloppily printed and bound in inexpensive paper. . . . In all reverence I say Heaven bless the Whodunit.
                          —Dorothy Parker

You cannot prevent the birds of sorrow from flying over your head, but you can prevent them from building nests in your hair. —CHINESE PROVERB

A man would prefer to come home to an unmade bed and a happy woman than to a neatly made bed and an angry woman. —MARLENE DIETRICH

When I ask myself, "Who are the happiest people on the planet?" my answer is, "Those who can't wait to wake up in the morning to get back to what they were doing the day before." —JAMES CRONIN

You see how diminutive your life and concerns are compared to other things in the universe. . . . The result is that you enjoy the life that is before you. . . . It allows you to have inner peace.
—EDWARD GIBSON, Skylab astronaut,
on viewing Earth from space

Puritanism: The haunting fear that someone, somewhere, may be happy.

—H. L. MENCKEN

To be really happy and really safe, one ought to have at least two or three hobbies, and they must all be real.

—WINSTON CHURCHILL

Earth will swing on its ellipse whatever you do, and crocuses will come up. The poets say happiness comes like this, though we cannot see the works. It is coming.

—JENNIFER MICHAEL HECHT

I urge you to please notice when you are happy, and exclaim or think or murmur at some point: "If this isn't nice, I don't know what is."   —KURT VONNEGUT

To make others less happy is a crime. To make ourselves unhappy is where all crime starts. We must try to contribute joy to the world. That is true no matter what our problems, our health, our circumstances. We must try.

—ROGER EBERT

No pleasure is comparable to the standing upon the vantage ground of truth (a hill not to be commanded, and where the air is always clear and serene), and to see the errors, and wanderings, and mists, and tempests, in the vale below; so always that this prospect be with pity, and not with swelling, or pride. Certainly, it is heaven upon earth, to have a man's mind move in charity, rest in providence, and turn upon the poles of truth.

—FRANCIS BACON

It was one of those jolly, peaceful mornings that make a chappie wish he'd got a soul or something.

—P. G. WODEHOUSE,
"Jeeves and the Hard-Boiled Egg"

There is only one inborn error, and that is the notion that we exist in order to be happy. . . . We are nothing more than the will-to-live, and the successive satisfaction of all our willing is what we think of through the concept of happiness.   —ARTHUR SCHOPENHAUER

Happiness is good health and a bad memory.

—INGRID BERGMAN

I have an idea, a theory, that what seem small things are perhaps the only things in life to help the big things. For instance, a hot bath. I can't think of any sorrow in the world that a hot bath wouldn't help, just a little bit.

—SUSAN GLASPELL, *The Visioning*

If one only wished to be happy, this could be easily accomplished; but we wish to be happier than other people, and this is always difficult, for we believe others to be happier than they are.   —CHARLES DE MONTESQUIEU

A vigorous five-mile walk will do more good for an unhappy but otherwise healthy adult than all the medicine and psychology in the world.   —PAUL DUDLEY WHITE

If you observe a really happy man, you will find him building a boat, writing a symphony, educating his son, growing double dahlias in his garden, or looking for dinosaur eggs in the Gobi desert. He will not be searching for happiness as if it were a collar stud that has rolled under the dressing-table. —W. BERAN WOLFE

It is neither wealth nor splendour, but tranquility and occupation, which give happiness.

—THOMAS JEFFERSON

A morning-glory at my window satisfies me more than the metaphysics of books.

—WALT WHITMAN, "Song of Myself"

One of the distinguishing marks of true adventures . . . is that they were often not fun at all while they were actually happening. —KIM STANLEY ROBINSON

I have love, blue skies, rainbows, and Hallmark cards, and that has to be enough. It has to be enough, but it's everything in the world, and everything in the world is plenty for me. It seems just rude to beg the invisible for more. —PENN JILLETTE

Maybe life itself is the proper binge.

—JULIA CHILD

Man had always assumed that he was more intelligent than dolphins because he had achieved so much—the wheel, New York, wars and so on—whilst all the dolphins had ever done was muck about in the water having a good time. But conversely, the dolphins had always believed that they were far more intelligent than man— for precisely the same reasons.

—Douglas Adams,
The Hitchhiker's Guide to the Galaxy

Being satisfied with what we already have is a magical golden key to being alive in a full, unrestricted, and inspired way.   —Pema Chödrön

Happiness comes in small doses folks. It's a cigarette, or a chocolate chip cookie or a five second orgasm, that's it, OK? You come, you eat the cookie, you smoke the butt, you go to sleep, you get up in the morning and go to fucking work, OK? That is it, end of fucking list.

—Denis Leary

The fact that a believer is happier than a skeptic is no more to the point than the fact that a drunken man is happier than a sober one. The happiness of credulity is a cheap and dangerous quality of happiness, and by no means a necessity of life.   —GEORGE BERNARD SHAW

It is vain to ask of the gods what a man is capable of supplying for himself.   —EPICURUS

There are something like 18 billion cells in the brain alone. There are no two brains alike; there are no two hands alike; there are no two human beings alike. You can take your instructions and your guidance from others, but you must find your own path.
     —JOSEPH CAMPBELL

It's an experience like no other experience I can describe, the best thing that can happen to a scientist, realizing that something that's happened in his or her mind exactly corresponds to something that happens in nature. It's startling every time it occurs. One is surprised that a construct of one's own mind can actually be realized in the honest-to-goodness world out there. A great shock, and a great, great joy.   —LEO KADANOFF

I did not believe that a Cause which stood for a beautiful ideal, for anarchism, for release and freedom from convention and prejudice, should demand the denial of life and joy.   —EMMA GOLDMAN

Religion is a story that the left brain tells the right brain. . . . Nirvana exists right now. There is no doubt that it is a beautiful state and that we can get there.
                                        —JILL BOLTE TAYLOR

The existence of vastly more great books than I can ever hope to read is a primary locus of joy in this life, and weight on the scale in favor of human civilization.
                                        —JONATHAN LETHEM

[Humankind] in its poverty, has unquestionably one really effective weapon—laughter. Power, Money, Persuasion, Supplication, Persecution—these can lift at a colossal humbug,—push it a little—crowd it a little—weaken it a little, century by century: but only Laughter can blow it to rags and atoms at a blast. Against the assault of Laughter nothing can stand.
                                        —MARK TWAIN, *The Mysterious Stranger*

The mother of excess is not joy but joylessness.
                                        —FRIEDRICH NIETZSCHE

And I find . . . nothing more noble than the history of our struggle to understand nature—a majestic entity of such vast spatial and temporal scope that she cannot care

much for a little mammalian afterthought with a curious evolutionary invention, even if that invention has,
for the first time in some four billion years of life on
earth, produced recursion as a creature reflects back
upon its own production and evolution.

—STEPHEN JAY GOULD

What sky! What light! Ah, in spite of all it is a blessed
thing to be alive in such weather, and out of hospital.

—SAMUEL BECKETT, *All That Fall*

Human Nature

Naughtiness is rare. Most people are too much absorbed in themselves to be bad. —Friedrich Nietzsche

If the world were merely seductive . . . that would be easy. If it were merely challenging, that would be no problem. But I arise in the morning torn between a desire to improve (or save) the world and a desire to enjoy (or savor) the world. This makes it hard to plan the day. —E. B. White

Streets are straight, houses are square, and our bodies are round. We don't belong there. We belong outside, doing stuff. —Warren Miller

The real problem of humanity is the following: we have Paleolithic emotions; medieval institutions; and god-like technology. —E. O. Wilson

A man is a worker. If he is not that he is nothing. . . . For the great mass of mankind the only saving grace that is needed is steady fidelity to what is nearest to hand and heart in the short moment of each human effort.

—JOSEPH CONRAD

Each of us must make his own true way, and when we do, that way will express the universal way.

—SHUNRYU SUZUKI ROSHI

As long as the world is turning and spinning, we're gonna be dizzy and we're gonna make mistakes.

—MEL BROOKS, *The 2,000 Year Old Man*

Poison's not bad. It's a matter of how much.

—KEITH RICHARDS

Our tools are better than we are, and grow better faster than we do. They suffice to crack the atom, to command the tides, but they do not suffice for the oldest task in human history, to live on a piece of land without spoiling it.

—ALDO LEOPOLD

Never trust a man who, when left alone in a room with a tea-cozy, doesn't try it on.   —BILLY CONNOLLY

My dear Kepler, what would you say of the learned here, who, replete with the pertinacity of the asp, have steadfastly refused to cast a glance through the telescope? What shall we make of this? Shall we laugh, or shall we cry?
—GALILEO GALILEI, in a letter to Johannes Kepler

They tried to get me to hate white people, but someone would always come along & spoil it.
—THELONIOUS MONK

A human being should be able to change a diaper, plan an invasion, butcher a hog, conn a ship, design a building, write a sonnet, balance accounts, build a wall, set a bone, comfort the dying, take orders, give orders, cooperate, act alone, solve equations, analyze a new problem, pitch manure, program a computer, cook a tasty meal, fight efficiently, die gallantly. Specialization is for insects.   —ROBERT A. HEINLEIN, *Time Enough for Love*

There are only two or three human stories, and they go on repeating themselves as fiercely as if they had never happened before; like the larks in this country, that have been singing the same five notes over for thousands of years.   —WILLA CATHER, *O Pioneers!*

After all, human beings are like that. When they are alone they want to be with others, and when they are with others they want to be alone.   —GERTRUDE STEIN

We would not be here if humanity were inherently evil. We'd have eaten ourselves alive long ago. So when you spot violence, or bigotry, or intolerance or fear or just garden-variety misogyny, hatred or ignorance, just look it in the eye and think, "The good outnumber you, and we always will."   —PATTON OSWALT

Most people would die sooner than think—in fact they do so.

—BERTRAND RUSSELL

We want to be special in a universe that is uncaring and cold, and in which the nature of our existence is a transient flicker, so we invent these strange stories of grand beginnings, like every orphan dreaming that they are the children of kings who will one day ride up on a white horse and take them away to a beautiful palace and a rich and healthy family that will love them forever. We are not princes of the earth, we are the descendants of worms, and any nobility must be earned.

—PZ MYERS

Humans are able to count because the world contains countable things (like stars, stones, and seasons) that can be put in successive correspondence with one another, and because the mind evolved to capture what the universe contains so that the organism that carried this representational tool (the mind) could survive and reproduce. —SCOTT ATRAN

Although many of us may think of ourselves as *thinking creatures that feel*, biologically we are *feeling creatures that think*. —JILL BOLTE TAYLOR

If somebody'd said before the flight, "Are you going to get carried away looking at the earth from the moon?" I would have said, "No, no way." But yet when I first looked back at the earth, standing on the moon, I cried.
—ALAN SHEPARD, NASA astronaut and first American to travel into space

Man, you might say, is nature dreaming.
—ROBINSON JEFFERS, "The Beauty of Things"

To state quite simply what we learn in a time of pestilence: that there are more things to admire in men than to despise. —ALBERT CAMUS, *The Plague*

Wars and armies and nuclear weapons are essentially heterosexual hobbies. —MORRISSEY

Most of our ancestors were not perfect ladies and gentlemen. The majority of them weren't even mammals.
—ROBERT ANTON WILSON

Not being funny doesn't make you a bad person. Not
having a sense of humor does.   —DAVID RAKOFF

There are two kinds of people in this world: those who
know where their high school yearbook is and those
who do not.   —SLOANE CROSLEY

There is nothing at all absurd about the human condition. We matter . . . we may be engaged in the formation
of something like a mind for the life of this planet. If this
is so, we are still at the most primitive stage, still fum-
bling with language and thinking, but infinitely capaci-
tated for the future. Looked at this way, it is remarkable
that we have come as far as we have in so short a period,
really no time at all as geologists measure time. We are
the newest, the youngest, and the brightest thing around.
—LEWIS THOMAS

Science is used to raise money for the expeditions, but
you really climb for the hell of it.
—SIR EDMUND HILLARY

Man is the only animal that laughs and weeps, for he is the only animal that is struck with the difference between what things are, and what they ought to be.

—WILLIAM HAZLITT

Language was invented to ask questions. Answers may be given by grunts and gestures, but questions must be spoken. Humanness came of age when man asked the first question.

—ERIC HOFFER

But it does me no injury for my neighbors to say there are twenty gods, or no god. It neither picks my pocket nor breaks my leg.

—THOMAS JEFFERSON

What a strange machine man is! You fill him with bread, wine, fish and radishes, and out come sighs, laughter and dreams.

—NIKOS KAZANTZAKIS, *Zorba the Greek*

Although attempting to bring about world peace through the internal transformation of individuals is difficult, it is the only way.

—TENZIN GYATSO, the 14th Dalai Lama

He who makes a beast of himself gets rid of the pain of being a man.

—SAMUEL JOHNSON

Humor

A sense of humor is a measurement of the extent to which we realize that we are trapped in a world almost totally devoid of reason. Laughter is how we express the anxiety we feel at this knowledge.   —DAVE BARRY

They say rather than cursing the darkness, one should light a candle. They don't mention anything about cursing a lack of candles.   —GEORGE CARLIN

You can make fun of everything.   —MATT STONE

Irreverence is easy—what's hard is wit.   —TOM LEHRER

Even though laughter may well be "the best medicine," it is not, in point of fact, actual medicine.
      —DAVID RAKOFF

Laugh at what you hold sacred, and still hold it sacred.
      —ABRAHAM MASLOW

Seriousness is no more a guarantee of truth, insight, authenticity or probity, than humor is a guarantee of superficiality and stupidity.   —STEPHEN FRY

I was delighted too when I heard about the Nobel Prize, thinking as you did that my bongo playing was at last recognized.   —RICHARD P. FEYNMAN

If you ever start taking life too seriously, just remember that we are talking monkeys on an organic spaceship flying through the universe.   —JOE ROGAN

> Don't take life so serious . . . it ain't nohow permanent.
>
> —WALT KELLY, *Pogo*

Ideas and Knowledge

The only thing more dangerous than an idea is a belief.
—SARAH VOWELL

Dare to know! (*Sapere aude*.) "Have the courage to use your own understanding," is therefore the motto of the enlightenment.
—IMMANUEL KANT

Anti-intellectualism—the fear and distrust of thinking people—is a disease we must simply stamp out, just as we've stamped out smallpox and typhoid and polio.
—HUBERT HUMPHREY

We can be absolutely certain only about things we do not understand.
—ERIC HOFFER

The point of philosophy is to start with something so simple as not to seem worth stating, and to end with something so paradoxical that no one will believe it.
—BERTRAND RUSSELL

Bombs and pistols do not make a revolution. The sword of revolution is sharpened on the whetting-stone of ideas.
                                              —BHAGAT SINGH

We must think critically, and not just about the ideas of others. Be hard on your beliefs. Take them out onto the verandah and beat them with a cricket bat.
                                              —TIM MINCHIN

In the history of physics, every time we've looked beyond the scales and energies we were familiar with, we've found things that we wouldn't have thought were there. You look inside the atom and eventually you discover quarks. Who would have thought that? It's hubris to think that the way we see things is everything there is.
                                              —LISA RANDALL

Why can't somebody give us a list of things that everybody thinks and nobody says, and another list of things that everybody says and nobody thinks?
                                              —OLIVER WENDELL HOLMES, SR.

The mind of man is capable of anything—because everything is in it, all the past as well as all the future.
                                  —JOSEPH CONRAD, *Heart of Darkness*

The intellectual life of man, his culture and history and religion and science, is different from anything else we know of in the universe. That is fact. It is as if all life evolved to a certain point, and then ourselves turned at a right angle and simply exploded in a different direction.

—JULIAN JAYNES

The universe consists primarily of dark matter. We can't see it, but it has an enormous gravitational force. The conscious mind—much like the visible aspect of the universe—is only a small fraction of the mental world. The dark matter of the mind, the unconscious, has the greatest psychic gravity. Disregard the dark matter of the universe and anomalies appear. Ignore the dark matter of the mind and our irrationality is inexplicable.

—JOEL GOLD

Books and opinions, no matter from whom they came, if they are in opposition to human rights, are nothing but dead letters.

—ERNESTINE ROSE

Those who read own the world, and those who watch television lose it.

—WERNER HERZOG

What progress we are making. In the Middle Ages they would have burned me. Now they are content with burning my books.

—SIGMUND FREUD

The effort to understand the universe is one of the very few things which lifts human life a little above the level of farce and gives it some of the grace of tragedy.

—STEVEN WEINBERG

If you want to have good ideas you must have many ideas. Most of them will be wrong, and what you have to learn is which ones to throw away.   —LINUS PAULING

Overcoming naive impressions to figure out how things really work is one of humanity's highest callings.

—STEVEN PINKER

Bid farewell to ideologies and instead return to the truth of being human.   —GAO XINGJIAN

I can't understand why people are frightened of new ideas. I'm frightened of the old ones.

—JOHN CAGE

I know nothing except the fact of my own ignorance.

—SOCRATES

The only way I can tell that a new idea is really important is the feeling of terror that seizes me.

—JAMES FRANCK

We used to think that if we knew one, we knew two, because one and one are two. We are finding that we must learn a great deal more about "and."

—Sir Arthur Eddington

Contradiction is the essence of the universe.

—Fernando Pessoa

So in the end when one is doing philosophy one gets to the point where one would just like to emit an inarticulate sound.

—Ludwig Wittgenstein

There is nothing so absurd that some philosopher has not said it.

—Cicero

All you have to do to educate a child is leave him alone and teach him to read. The rest is brainwashing.

—Ellen Gilchrist

A formal manipulator in mathematics often experiences the discomforting feeling that his pencil surpasses him in intelligence.

—Howard W. Eves

The most technologically efficient machine that man ever invented is the book.

—Northrop Frye

When someone says that life would not exist if the laws of physics were just a little bit different, I have to wonder ... *how do they know?* Just as there are many different combinations of amino acids that can make any particular enzyme, why can't there be many different combinations of physical laws that can yield life? Do the experiment of testing different universes, then come talk to me.
—PZ MYERS

Man can learn nothing except by going from the known into the unknown.
—CLAUDE BERNARD

The capacity for discerning the essential truth, in fact, is as rare among men as it is common among crows, bull-frogs, and mackerel.
—H. L. MENCKEN

You know everybody is ignorant, only on different sub-jects.
—WILL ROGERS

Let us reflect that [the Earth] is inhabited by a thousand millions of people. That these profess probably a thousand different systems of religion. That ours is but one of that thousand. That if there be but one right, and ours that one, we should wish to see the 999 wandering sects gathered into the fold of truth. But against such a majority we cannot effect this by force. Reason and persuasion are the only practicable instruments. To make way for these, free enquiry must be indulged; and how can we wish others to indulge it while we refuse it ourselves?

—THOMAS JEFFERSON

Man is always ready to die for an idea, provided that the idea is not quite clear to him. —PAUL ELDRIDGE

The future is disorder. A door like this has cracked open five or six times since we got up on our hind legs. It's the best possible time to be alive, when almost everything you thought you knew was wrong.

—TOM STOPPARD, *Arcadia*

A system that makes no errors is not intelligent.

—GERD GIGERENZER

Identity

Be plural like the universe.　　　　—FERNANDO PESSOA

A man becomes his attentions. His observations and curiosity, they make and remake him.
　　　　　　　　　—WILLIAM LEAST HEAT-MOON

Nonconformity is the highest evolutionary attainment of social animals.　　　　　　　　—ALDO LEOPOLD

I don't know what I'm like. It's the only thing we can never know.　　　　　　　　　—JANE CAMPION

The electric meat! That's us. . . . If anything, it's even more awe-inspiring to think that out of physics and chemistry we're able to get consciousness and thought.
　　　　—MICHAEL SHERMER, when asked if "humans are
　　　　　　　just products of physics and chemistry"

To assign unanswered letters their proper weight, to free us from the expectations of others, to give us back to ourselves—there lies the great, the singular power of self-respect. Without it, one eventually discovers the final turn of the screw: one runs away to find oneself, and finds no one at home. —JOAN DIDION

The self is not so much linked to its ancestors . . . but rather, in the strictest sense of the word, the same thing as all that: the strict, direct continuation of it, just as the self aged fifty is the continuation of the self aged forty. —ERWIN SCHRÖDINGER

What they call you is one thing. What you answer to is something else.

—LUCILLE CLIFTON

Sometimes it happens that a man's circle of horizon becomes smaller and smaller, and as the radius approaches zero it concentrates on one point. And then that becomes his point of view. —DAVID HILBERT

You are an intelligent human being. Your life is valuable for its own sake. You are not second-class in the universe, deriving meaning and purpose from some other mind. You are not inherently evil—you are inherently human, possessing the positive rational potential to help

make this a world of morality, peace and joy. Trust yourself.   —Dan Barker

Each of us is a singular narrative, which is constructed,
continually, unconsciously, by, through, and in us. . . .
Biologically, physiologically, we are not so different from
each other; historically, as narratives—we are each of us
unique.   —Oliver Sacks

To the dumb question "Why me?" the cosmos barely
bothers to return the reply: Why not?
                                      —Christopher Hitchens

I have heard many people speak of who they believe they
were in previous incarnations, but they seem to have
very little idea of who they are in this one. . . . Let's take
one life at a time. Perhaps the best way to do that is to
live as though there were no afterlife or reincarnation.
To live as though this moment was all that was allotted.
                                          —Stephen Levine

You and I are all as much continuous with the physical
universe as a wave is continuous with the ocean.
                                              —Alan Watts

We did not ask to be born. We are not committed to
those who bore us. We are in our own elemental rela-
tionship to the sources of life. We belong to ourselves.
                                      —Kenneth L. Patton

He did not make any concessions, period. That, to me—in addition to the carrying of grudges—is the definition of character. —FRAN LEBOWITZ, on the writer James Purdy

I know that personality is just an invention of the news media. I know that character exists from the outside alone. I know that inside the body there's just temperature. —SHEILA HETI, *How Should a Person Be?*

Any life, no matter how long and complex it may be, is made up of a single moment: the moment in which a man finds out, once and for all, who he is.

—JORGE LUIS BORGES,
"A Biography of Tadeo Isidoro Cruz"

People seem not to see that their opinion of the world is also a confession of character.

—RALPH WALDO EMERSON

A faculty for idleness implies a catholic appetite and a strong sense of personal identity.

—ROBERT LOUIS STEVENSON

The serial number of the human specimen is the face, that accidental and unrepeatable combination of features. It reflects neither character nor soul nor what we call the self. —MILAN KUNDERA, *Immortality*

> *My own mind is my own church.*
>
> —THOMAS PAINE

All beings alive today are equally evolved. All have survived over three thousand million years of evolution from common bacterial ancestors. There are no "higher" beings, no "lower animals," no angels, and no gods. . . . Human similarities to other life forms are far more striking than the differences. Our deep connections, over vast geological periods, should inspire awe, not repulsion.   —LYNN MARGULIS

I am an abyss that I am trying to cross.
                    —W. S. MERWIN, "Abyss"

When I got untethered from the comfort of religion, it wasn't a loss of faith for me. It was a discovery of self. I had thought that I'm capable enough to handle any situation. There's peace in understanding that I have only one life, here and now, and I'm responsible.   —BRAD PITT

Man's character is his destiny.   —HERACLITUS

Damaged people are dangerous. They know they can survive.   —JOSEPHINE HART, *Damage*

Self-sufficiency is the greatest of all wealth.

—Epicurus

Now, nothing should be able to harm a man except himself. Nothing should be able to rob a man at all. What a man really has, is what is in him. What is outside of him should be a matter of no importance.   —Oscar Wilde

We are all alone, born alone, die alone, and—in spite of *True Romance* magazines—we shall all someday look back on our lives and see that, in spite of our company, we were alone the whole way. I do not say lonely—at least, not all the time—but essentially, and finally, alone. That is what makes self-respect so important, and I don't see how you can respect yourself if you must look in the hearts and minds of others for your happiness.

—Hunter S. Thompson

Ignorance more frequently begets confidence than does knowledge: it is those who know little, and not those who know much, who so positively assert that this or that problem will never be solved by science.

—Charles Darwin

Style is knowing who you are, what you want to say, and not giving a damn.   —Gore Vidal

If you don't have self-esteem, you will hesitate before you do anything in your life. You will hesitate to go for the job you want to go for. You will hesitate to ask for a raise. You will hesitate to call yourself an American. You will hesitate to report a rape. You will hesitate to defend yourself when you are discriminated against because of your race, your sexuality, your size, your gender. You will hesitate to vote; you will hesitate to dream. For us to have self-esteem is truly an act of revolution, and our revolution is long overdue.　　　—MARGARET CHO

Nothing is better for self-esteem than survival.
　　　　　　　　　　　　　　　—MARTHA GELLHORN

Some part of our being knows [the cosmos] is where we came from. We long to return. And we can. Because the cosmos is also within us. We're made of star-stuff. We are a way for the cosmos to know itself.
　　　　　　　　　　　　　　　—CARL SAGAN

Kindness

I respect kindness to human beings first of all, and kindness to animals. I don't respect the law; I have a total irreverence for anything concerned with society except that which makes the roads safer, the beer stronger, the food cheaper, and old men and women warmer in the winter and happier in the summer.

—Brendan Behan

If you can't be kind, at least be vague.

—Judith Martin, aka Miss Manners (attributed)

I have something that I call my Golden Rule. It goes something like this: "Do unto others twenty-five percent better than you expect them to do unto you." . . . The twenty-five percent is for error. —Linus Pauling

I shall go down and be very kind to everyone. Noble deeds and hot baths are the best cures for depression.

—Dodie Smith, *I Capture the Castle*

They call us romantics, weak, stupid, sentimental ideal-
ists, perhaps because we have some faith in the good
which exists even in our opponents and because we believe that kindness achieves more than cruelty.

—FRIDTJOF NANSEN

"Kindness" covers all of my political beliefs.

—ROGER EBERT

Shall we make a new rule of life from tonight: always to
try to be a little kinder than is necessary?

—J. M. BARRIE, *The Little White Bird*

My religion is very simple—my religion is kindness.

—TENZIN GYATSO, the 14th Dalai Lama

It's a little embarrassing that, after forty-five years of research and study, the best advice I can give to people is to
be a little kinder to each other.

—ALDOUS HUXLEY

Three things in human life are important.
The first is to be kind. The second is to be kind.
And the third is to be kind.

—WILLIAM JAMES

If we could read the secret history of our enemies, we should find in each man's life sorrow and suffering enough to disarm all hostility.

—HENRY WADSWORTH LONGFELLOW

That's one of the things the illness has given me: It's a degree of death. . . . Once you can accept that, you can accept anything. So then I think, Well, given that that's the case, let's tip myself a break. Let's tip everybody a break.

—MICHAEL J. FOX

Life teaches us to be less harsh with ourselves and with others.

—JOHANN WOLFGANG VON GOETHE

I have found that the only thing that does bring you happiness is doing something good for somebody who is incapable of doing it for themselves.

—DAVID LETTERMAN

Let's all give each other a pass, shall we?

—DAVID RAKOFF

Life

There is no wealth but life.   —JOHN RUSKIN

Life divides into AMAZING ENJOYABLE TIMES
and APPALLING EXPERIENCES THAT WILL
MAKE FUTURE AMAZING ANECDOTES.
                                    —CAITLIN MORAN

The most salient feature of existence is the unthinkable
odds against it. For every way that there is of being here,
there are an infinity of ways of not being here. Statistics
declare us ridiculous. Thermodynamics prohibits us.
Life, by any reasonable measure, is impossible.
        —RICHARD POWERS, *Generosity: An Enhancement*

Hope for the best. Expect the worst. / Life is a play. We're
unrehearsed.   —MEL BROOKS, *The Twelve Chairs*

Looking outward to the blackness of space, sprinkled
with the glory of a universe of lights, I saw majesty—but

no welcome. Below was a welcoming planet. There, contained in the thin, moving, incredibly fragile shell of the biosphere is everything that is dear to you, all the human drama and comedy. That's where life is; that's were all the good stuff is.

—Loren Acton, American Space Shuttle astronaut

We all have a better guide in ourselves, if we would attend to it, than any other person can be.

—Jane Austen, *Mansfield Park*

When a person is born, he can embark on only one of three roads of life: if you go right, the wolves will eat you; if you go left, you'll eat the wolves; if you go straight, you'll eat yourself.

—Anton Chekhov, *Fatherlessness*

After I stopped believing in God, I realized it was completely up to me to create my own meaning and my purpose was my own. God didn't care if I was working at the gas station my whole life or writing great novels. It didn't really matter in the universe what I did, but it mattered to me. —Julia Sweeney

One of the goals of education should be to teach that life is precious. —Abraham Maslow

Life is without meaning. You bring meaning to it. The meaning of life is whatever you ascribe it to be. Being alive is the meaning. —JOSEPH CAMPBELL

Spontaneous creation is the reason why there is something rather than nothing, why the universe exists, why we exist. —STEPHEN HAWKING

It is hard to master both life and work equally well. So if you are bound to fake one of them, it had better be life. —JOSEPH BRODSKY

Life cannot be meaningless so long as we have the capacity to affect the well-being of ourselves and others. —PAULA KIRBY

Women get more radical with age. —GLORIA STEINEM and PHYLLIS ROSSER

The main effort of arranging your life should be to progressively reduce the amount of time required to decently maintain yourself so that you can have all the time you want for reading. —NORMAN RUSH, *Mating*

I don't know why we live—the gift of life comes to us from I don't know what source or for what purpose; but I believe we can go on living for the reason that (always of course up to a certain point) life is the most valuable thing we know anything about and it is therefore presumptively a great mistake to surrender it while there is any yet left in the cup.　　　　　　　—HENRY JAMES

We die. That may be the meaning of life. But we do language. That may be the measure of our lives.
　　　　　　　　　　　　　　　　　—TONI MORRISON

A new dress doesn't get you anywhere; it's the life you're living in the dress, and the sort of life you had lived before, and what you will do in it later.
　　　　　　　　　　　　　　　　　—DIANA VREELAND

I have no faith, only a suitcaseful of beliefs that sustain me. Life's meaning has always eluded me and I guess it always will. But I love it just the same.　　—E. B. WHITE

The word "holiday" comes from "holy day" and holy means "exalted and worthy of complete devotion." By that definition, all days are holy. Life is holy. Atheists have joy every day of the year, every holy day. We have the wonder and glory of life. We have joy in the world before the lord is come. We're not going for the promise of life after death; we're celebrating life before death. The smiles of children. The screaming, the bitching, the horrific whining of one's own children. . . . Sunsets, rock and roll, bebop, Jell-O, stinky cheese, and offensive jokes. For atheists, everything in the world is enough and every day is holy. Every day is an atheist holiday. It's a day that we're alive. —PENN JILLETTE

If you want my opinion on the mystery of life and all that, I can give it to you in a nutshell: The universe is like a safe to which there is a key. But the key is locked up in the safe. —PETER DE VRIES

It isn't length of life, but depth of life. —RALPH WALDO EMERSON

May you live all the days of your life.

—JONATHAN SWIFT

The art of life is more like the wrestler's art than the dancer's, in respect of this, that it should stand ready and firm to meet onsets which are sudden and unexpected. —MARCUS AURELIUS

For man the vast marvel is to be alive. For man as for flower and beast and bird the supreme triumph is to be most vividly, most perfectly alive. Whatever the unborn and the dead may know they cannot know the beauty, the marvel of being alive in the flesh. The dead may look after the afterwards. But the magnificent here and now of life in the flesh is ours alone, and ours only for a time. We ought to dance with rapture that we should be alive and in the flesh and part of the living incarnate cosmos.

—D. H. LAWRENCE

Life engenders life. Energy creates energy. It is by spending oneself that one becomes rich.

—SARAH BERNHARDT

When we compare the present life of man on earth with that time of which we have no knowledge, it seems to me like the swift flight of a single sparrow through the banqueting-hall where you are sitting at dinner on a winter's day with your thanes and eldermen. In the midst there is a comforting fire to warm the hall; outside the storms of winter rain or snow are raging. This sparrow flies swiftly in through one door of the hall, and out through another. While he is inside, he is safe from the winter storms; but after a moment of comfort, he vanishes from sight into the wintry world from which he came. Even so, man appears on earth for a little while; but of what went before this life or of what follows, we know nothing. —THE VENERABLE BEDE

The two entities who might enlighten us, the baby and the corpse, cannot do so. —E. M. FORSTER

We are born. We eat sweet potatoes. Then we die.

—EASTER ISLAND PROVERB

It makes me laugh to recall how I used to think . . . that it's possible to create your own happy, honest little world, in which you can live in peace and quiet, without mistakes, regret, or confusion, doing only good things in an unhurried and precise way. Ridiculous! It's impossible. . . . To live an honest life you have to strive hard, get involved, fight, make mistakes, begin something and give it up, begin again and give it up again, struggle endlessly, and suffer loss. As for tranquility—it's spiritual baseness.

—LEO TOLSTOY

What people commonly call Fate is, as a general rule, nothing but their own stupid and foolish conduct.

—ARTHUR SCHOPENHAUER

In fact, not a shred of evidence exists in favor of the argument that life is serious, though it is often hard and even terrible. And saying that, I am prompted to add what follows out of it: that since everything ends badly for us, in the inescapable catastrophe of death, it seems obvious that the first rule of life is to have a good time; and that the second rule of life is to hurt as few people as possible in the course of doing so. There is no third rule.

—BRENDAN GILL

How we spend our days is, of course, how we spend our lives. What we do with this hour, and that one, is what we are doing. —ANNIE DILLARD

Life is intrinsically, well, boring and dangerous at the same time. At any given moment, the floor may open up. Of course, it almost never does; that's what makes it so boring. —EDWARD GOREY

One life is enough for me. —ALBERT EINSTEIN

Perhaps our eyes are merely a blank film which is taken from us after our deaths to be developed elsewhere and screened as our life story in some infernal cinema or dispatched as microfilm into the sidereal void. —JEAN BAUDRILLARD

To none is life given in freehold; to all on lease. —LUCRETIUS

Life is something to do when you can't get to sleep. —FRAN LEBOWITZ

If my life were not a dangerous, painful experiment, if I did not constantly skirt the abyss and feel the void under my feet, my life would have no meaning and I would not have been able to write anything. —HERMANN HESSE

Will I leave a scratch on a rock? No. There are so many people who do magnificent, significant things, and I don't. But what difference does it make whether you're remembered 50 years from now? It's this life that you're leading. —DEEDA BLAIR

The point of being over forty is to fulfill the desires you've been harboring since you were seven.
—GUILLERMO DEL TORO

The older you are, the freer you are, as long as you last.
—DAVID BROWER

It's better to fade away like an old soldier than to burn out. . . . Making Sid Vicious a hero, Jim Morrison—it's garbage to me. I worship the people who survive. Gloria Swanson, Greta Garbo. —JOHN LENNON

One does not get better but different and older and that is always a pleasure. —GERTRUDE STEIN

Life, however long, will always be short.

—WISŁAWA SZYMBORSKA, "Our Ancestors' Short Lives"

You know, some people say life is short and that you could get hit by a bus at any moment and that you have to live each day like it's your last. Bullshit. Life is long. You're probably not gonna get hit by a bus. And you're gonna have to live with the choices you make for the next fifty years.   —CHRIS ROCK

Let us toast to animal pleasures, to escapism, to rain on the roof and instant coffee, to unemployment insurance and library cards, to absinthe and good-hearted land-lords, to music and warm bodies and contraceptives . . . and to the "good life," whatever it is and wherever it happens to be.   —HUNTER S. THOMPSON

However mean your life is, meet it and live it; do not shun it and call it hard names. It is not so bad as you are.
                                         —HENRY DAVID THOREAU

You don't get to choose how you're going to die, or when. You can only decide how you're going to live. Now.
                                                      —JOAN BAEZ

I prefer . . . the laughers, materialists, radicals, cynics, hedonists, atheists, sensualists, voluptuaries. They know that there is only one world, and that promotion of an afterlife deprives us of the enjoyment and benefit of the only one there is.   —MICHEL ONFRAY

When you consider the world with its wars, its banks, its malls, give me a hit of acid and a torn dress and let's go to the beach.

> —ANTON "REGGIE" DUNNIGAN,
> former member of the Cockettes

Life is short, short, brother! Ain't it the truth? And there is no other Ain't it the truth? You gotta rock that rainbow while you still got your youth! Oh! Ain't it the solid truth?   —E. Y. "YIP" HARBURG, "Ain't It the Truth"

"What is the meaning of life?" is a stupid question. Life just exists. You say to yourself, "I can't accept that I mean nothing so I have to find the meaning of life so that I shouldn't mean as little as I know I do." Subconsciously you know you're full of shit. I see life as a dance. Does a dance have to have a meaning? You're dancing because you enjoy it.   —JACKIE MASON

Stranger, here you will do well to tarry; here our highest good is pleasure.

> —Inscription on the gate of the Garden, the
> school founded by Epicurus ca. 300 BCE

I have a very simple creed: that life and joy and beauty are better than dusty death.   —BERTRAND RUSSELL

I don't believe in life after death, but I'd like to believe in life before death. —NATALIE ANGIER

We could stop being lost if we were to just stop trying to get out of the forest. Instead, we could pick some blueberries, sit beneath a tree, and start describing how the sun-dappled forest floor shimmers in the breeze. The initial horror of being lost utterly disappears when you come to believe fully that there is no town out there, beyond the forest, to which you are headed. If there is no release, no going home, then this must be home, this shimmering instant replete with blueberries.

—JENNIFER MICHAEL HECHT

Is not life a hundred times too short for us—to bore ourselves? —FRIEDRICH NIETZSCHE

If there is a sin against life, it consists perhaps not so much in despairing of life as in hoping for another life and in eluding the implacable grandeur of this life.

—ALBERT CAMUS

The great end of life is not knowledge, but action.

—T. H. HUXLEY

The true meaning of life is to plant trees under whose shade you do not expect to sit. —NELSON HENDERSON

Given something like death, what does it matter if one looks foolish now and then, or tries too hard, or cares too deeply? A shallow life creates a life as flat as a shadow.

—DIANE ACKERMAN

Prime numbers are what is left when you have taken all the patterns away. I think prime numbers are like life. They are very logical but you could never work out the rules, even if you spent all your time thinking about them.

—MARK HADDON, *The Curious Incident of the Dog in the Night-Time*

I've learned what I can control is whether I am going to a live a day in fear and depression and panic, or whether I am going to attack the day and make it feel as good a day, as wonderful a day, as I can. —GILDA RADNER

I'm not telling you to make the world better, because I don't think that progress is necessarily part of the package. I'm just telling you to live in it. Not just to endure it, not just to suffer it, not just to pass through it, but to live in it. To look at it. To try to get the picture. To live recklessly. To take chances. To make your own work and take pride in it. To seize the moment. And if you ask me why you should bother to do that, I could tell you that the grave's a fine and private place, but none I think do there embrace. Nor do they sing there, or write, or argue, or see the tidal bore on the Amazon, or touch their children. And that's what there is to do and get it while you can and good luck at it.　　—JOAN DIDION

What's to come is still unsure: / In delay there lies no plenty; / Then come kiss me, sweet and twenty! / Youth's a stuff will not endure. —WILLIAM SHAKESPEARE, *Twelfth Night*

Our obligation is to give meaning to life and in doing so to overcome the passive, indifferent life. A person who is indifferent is dead without knowing it. I believe that life has meaning in spite of the meaningless death I have seen. Death has no meaning, life has. We must make every minute rich and enriching, not for oneself, but for someone else, and thereby create a bridge between beings that limits the domain of nothingness. Life is a gift and meaning is its reward. The meaning of life is to be found in every encounter. Every moment is a moment of grace.　　—ELIE WIESEL

We are all here to see and contemplate the great spectacle . . . we are a part of the outcome of all these raging and conflicting forces. Whatever has failed, we have succeeded, and the beneficent forces are still coming our way.　　—JOHN BURROUGHS

The question is: What's the mill? Not: What's the grist?　　—PHILIP GLASS

I wish to live because life has that within it that which is good, that which is beautiful, and that which is love.

—LORRAINE HANSBERRY

The purpose of life is to stay alive. Watch any animal in nature—all it tries to do is stay alive. It doesn't care about beliefs or philosophy. Whenever any animal's behavior puts it out of touch with the realities of its existence, it becomes extinct.

—MICHAEL CRICHTON, *Congo*

Life is a tragedy when seen in close-up, but a comedy in long-shot.

—CHARLIE CHAPLIN

Philosophy is written in this grand book—I mean the universe—which stands continually open to our gaze, but it cannot be understood unless one first learns to comprehend the language in which it is written. It is written in the language of mathematics, and its characters are triangles, circles, and other geometric figures, without which it is humanly impossible to understand a single word of it; without these, one is wandering about in a dark labyrinth. —GALILEO GALILEI

The only reason for life is life. There is no why. We are. Life is beyond reason. One might think of life as a large organism, and we are but a small symbiotic part of it.

—GEORGE LUCAS

My life seemed to be a series of events and accidents. Yet when I look back I see a pattern.

—BENOIT MANDELBROT

Life has to be given a meaning because of the obvious fact that it has no meaning. —HENRY MILLER

What the meaning of human life may be I don't know: I incline to suspect that it has none. All I know about it is that, to me at least, it is very amusing while it lasts. Even its troubles, indeed, can be amusing. Moreover, they tend to foster the human qualities that I admire most—courage and its analogues.

—H. L. MENCKEN

It is the useless things that make life worth living and that make life dangerous too: wine, love, art, beauty. Without them life is safe but not worth bothering with.

—STEPHEN FRY

I think we are a part of something larger than ourselves. . . . We come from a very specific series of events in this universe, that if they hadn't happened, we wouldn't be here. . . . [A] cold, empty cosmos collapses with stars, and stars burn and shine, and they make carbon in their cores and then they throw them out again. And that carbon collects and forms another planet and another star and then amino acids evolve and then human beings arise. . . . That's, to me, a really beautiful narrative.   —JANNA LEVIN

No why. Just here.   —JOHN CAGE

If there is no point in the universe that we discover by the methods of science, there is a point that we can give the universe by the way we live, by loving each other, by discovering things about nature, by creating works of art. And that—in a way, although we are not the stars in a cosmic drama, if the only drama we're starring in is one that we are making up as we go along, it is not entirely ignoble that faced with this unloving, impersonal universe we make a little island of warmth and love and science and art for ourselves. That's not an entirely despicable role for us to play.   —STEVEN WEINBERG

Good taste is the excuse I've always given for leading such a bad life.   —OSCAR WILDE

I believe that I am not responsible for the meaningfulness or meaninglessness of life, but that I am responsible for what I do with the life I've got.

—HERMANN HESSE

If, after all, men cannot always make history have a meaning, they can always act so that their own lives have one. —ALBERT CAMUS

I meet a lot of people. And, see some great looking babes. And a fire engine goes by. And I give them the thumbs up. And, and ask a woman what kind of dog that is. And, and I don't know. The moral of the story is, is we're here on Earth to fart around. —KURT VONNEGUT

Life, if thou knowest how to use it, is long enough.

—SENECA

Life and love are life and love, a bunch of violets is a bunch of violets, and to drag in the idea of a point is to ruin everything. Live and let live, love and let love, flower and fade, and follow the natural curve, which flows on, pointless. —D. H. LAWRENCE

As far as we can discern, the sole purpose of human existence is to kindle a light of meaning in the darkness of mere being. —CARL JUNG

That life is worth living is the most necessary of assumptions, and were it not assumed, the most impossible of conclusions. —GEORGE SANTAYANA

We are here just for a spell and then pass on. So get a few laughs and do the best you can. Live your life so that whenever you lose it, you are ahead.   —WILL ROGERS

There is not one big cosmic meaning for all; there is only the meaning we each give to our life, an individual meaning, an individual plot, like an individual novel, a book for each person.   —ANAÏS NIN

To be what we are, and to become what we are capable of becoming, is the only end of life.
—ROBERT LOUIS STEVENSON

Because children grow up, we think a child's purpose is to grow up. But a child's purpose is to be a child. Nature doesn't disdain what lives only for a day. It pours the whole of itself into each moment. We don't value the lily less for not being made of flint and built to last. Life's bounty is in its flow, later is too late. Where is the song when it's been sung? The dance when it's been danced? It's only we humans who want to own the future, too. . . . Was the child happy while he lived? That is a proper question, the only question. If we can't arrange our own happiness, it's a conceit beyond vulgarity to arrange the happiness of those who come after us.

—Tom Stoppard, *The Coast of Utopia: Shipwreck*

All men should strive to learn before they die what they are running from, and to, and why.

—JAMES THURBER

Beyond work and love, I would add two other ingredients that give meaning to life. First, to fulfill whatever talents we are born with. However blessed we are by fate with different abilities and strengths, we should try to develop them to the fullest, rather than allow them to atrophy and decay. . . . Second, we should try to leave the world a better place than when we entered it. As individuals, we can make a difference, whether it is to probe the secrets of Nature, to clean up the environment and work for peace and social justice, or to nurture the inquisitive, vibrant spirit of the young by being a mentor and a guide. —Michio Kaku

Everyone seems to have a clear idea of how other people should lead their lives, but none about his or her own.

—Paulo Coelho, *The Alchemist*

Ye know full well that the meaning of life is to find your gift. To find your gift is happiness. Never tae find it is misery.   —TERRY PRATCHETT, *I Shall Wear Midnight*

A life that partakes even a little of friendship, love, irony, humor, parenthood, literature, and music, and the chance to take part in battles for the liberation of others cannot be called "meaningless" except if the person living it is also an existentialist and elects to call it so.
                                        —CHRISTOPHER HITCHENS

Well, it's nothing very special. Try to be nice to people, avoid eating fat, read a good book every now and then, get some walking in, and try and live together in peace and harmony with people of all creeds and nations.
                                        —"The End of the Film,"
                                        Monty Python's *The Meaning of Life*

The brave men, living and dead, who struggled here, have consecrated it far above our poor power to add or detract. The world will little note nor long remember what we say here, but it can never forget what they did here. It is for us, the living, rather, to be dedicated here to the unfinished work which they who fought here have thus far so nobly advanced.
                                        —ABRAHAM LINCOLN, Gettysburg Address

Love

All that you've loved is all you own.
> —Tom Waits, "Take It with Me"

Love does not rule, it cultivates. And that is more.
> —Johann Wolfgang von Goethe,
> *The Green Snake and the Beautiful Lily*

Love is not a desire for beauty; it is a yearning for completion.
> —Octavio Paz

To love another human in all of her splendor and imperfect perfection, it is a magnificent task . . . tremendous and foolish and human.
> —Louise Erdrich, *The Last Report on the Miracles at Little No Horse*

I say this is a wild dream—but it is this dream I want to realize. Life and literature combined, love the dynamo, you with your chameleon's soul giving me a thousand loves, being anchored always in no matter what storm, home wherever we are.

—HENRY MILLER, in a letter to Anaïs Nin

When I saw you I fell in love, and you smiled because you knew. —ARRIGO BOITO, *Falstaff*

The best thing you can possibly do with your life is to tackle the motherfucking shit out of love.

—CHERYL STRAYED

Perhaps the feelings that we experience when we are in love represent a normal state. Being in love shows a person who he should be. —ANTON CHEKHOV

And don't worry about losing [love]. If it is right, it happens—The main thing is not to hurry. Nothing good gets away. —JOHN STEINBECK

Man has conquered whole nations, but all his armies could not conquer love. Man has chained and fettered the spirit, but he has been utterly helpless before love.

—EMMA GOLDMAN

I urge you all today, especially today in these times of terrorism and chaos to love yourselves without reservation and to love each other without restraint. Unless you're into leather; then by all means, use restraints.

—MARGARET CHO

Not every problem that someone has with his girlfriend is necessarily due to the capitalist mode of production.

—HERBERT MARCUSE

Being with you and not being with you is the only way I have to measure time.

—JORGE LUIS BORGES, "The Threatened One"

The true beloveds of this world are in their lover's eyes, lilacs opening, ship lights, school bells, a landscape, remembered conversations, friends, a child's Sunday, lost voices, one's favorite suit, autumn and all seasons, memory, yes, it being the earth and water of existence, memory.   —TRUMAN CAPOTE, *Other Voices, Other Rooms*

Love is a snowmobile racing across the tundra and then suddenly it flips over, pinning you underneath. At night, the ice weasels come.

—MATT GROENING, *Love Is Hell*

Love takes off masks that we fear we cannot live without and know we cannot live within.   —JAMES BALDWIN

Love is the extremely difficult realisation that something other than oneself is real. Love, and so art and morals, is the discovery of reality. —IRIS MURDOCH

> *You cannot save people,*
> *you can only love them.*
>
> —ANAÏS NIN

Nothing is far and nothing is near, if one desires. The world is little, people are little, human life is little. There is only one big thing—desire. And before it, when it is big, all is little. —WILLA CATHER, *The Song of the Lark*

I don't think there's any difference between a crush and profound love. I think the experience is that you dissolve your sentries and your battalions for a moment and you really do see that there is this unfixed, free-flowing energy of emotion and thought between people. It's tangible and you can almost ride it onto another person's breast. —LEONARD COHEN

Say I love you, to those you love. The eternal silence is long enough to be silent in, and that awaits us all. —GEORGE ELIOT

I tell you, the more I think, the more I feel that there is nothing more truly artistic than to love people.

—VINCENT VAN GOGH

No matter what you're feeling, the only way to get a difficult feeling to go away is simply to love yourself for it. If you think you're stupid, then love yourself for feeling that way. It's a paradox, but it works. To heal, you must be the first one to shine the light of compassion on any areas within you that you feel are unacceptable.

—CHRISTIANE NORTHRUP

LOVE is anterior to life,
Posterior to death,
Initial of creation, and
The exponent of breath.

—EMILY DICKINSON, Poem #37

For small creatures such as we the vastness is bearable only through love.

—CARL SAGAN

Morality

There are far too many commandments and you really only need one: Do not hurt anybody. —CARL REINER

I stopped believing there was a power of good and a power of evil that were outside us. And I came to believe that good and evil are names for what people do, not for what they are. —PHILIP PULLMAN, *The Amber Spyglass*

The superior man understands what is right; the inferior man understands what will sell. —CONFUCIUS

The greatest tragedy in mankind's entire history may be the hijacking of morality by religion.
 —ARTHUR C. CLARKE

Until the lions have their own historians, the history of the hunt will always glorify the hunter.
 —CHINUA ACHEBE, paraphrasing an African proverb

If you don't stick to your values when they're being tested, they're not values—they're hobbies.

—JON STEWART

If I had a large amount of money I should certainly found a hospital for those whose grip upon the world is so tenuous that they can be severely offended by words and phrases and yet remain all unoffended by the injustice, violence and oppression that howls daily about our ears.

—STEPHEN FRY

The fact that a belief has a good moral effect upon a man is no evidence whatsoever in favor of its truth.

—BERTRAND RUSSELL

I believe the only reality is how we treat each other. The morality comes from the absence of any grander scheme, not from the presence of any grander scheme.

—JOSS WHEDON

Equality is not the empirical claim that all groups of humans are interchangeable; it is the moral principle that individuals should not be judged or constrained by the average properties of their group.

—STEVEN PINKER

If we're going to live an ethical life, it's not enough just to follow the thou-shalt-nots. . . . If we have enough, we

have to share some of that with people who have so
little. —PETER SINGER

All the world's major religions, with their emphasis on
love, compassion, patience, tolerance, and forgiveness
can and do promote inner values. But the reality of the
world today is that grounding ethics in religion is no
longer adequate. This is why I am increasingly con-
vinced that the time has come to find a way of thinking
about spirituality and ethics beyond religion altogether.
—TENZIN GYATSO, the 14th Dalai Lama

The one and only test of a valid religious idea, doctrinal
statement, spiritual experience, or devotional practice
was that it must lead directly to practical compassion.
—KAREN ARMSTRONG

I'm not a believer in predetermined fates, being re-
warded for one's efforts. I'm not a believer in karma.
The reason why I try to be a good person is because I
think it's the right thing to do. If I commit fewer bad acts
there will be fewer bad acts, maybe other people will join
in committing fewer bad acts, and in time there will be
fewer and fewer of them. —DANIEL HANDLER

We must always take sides. Neutrality helps the oppres-
sor, never the victim. Silence encourages the tormentor,
never the tormented. Sometimes we must interfere.
—ELIE WIESEL

From time to time I try to suggest that we weren't as heroic as people make us out to be. It would be more analytically precise, it seems to me, to say that we did the only thing we could do under the circumstances, short of Behaving like complete shits.

—RING LARDNER, JR., who was professionally blacklisted in Hollywood and sent to prison for 12 months for refusing to testify at the House Un-American Activities Committee in 1947

The only lies for which we are truly punished are those we tell ourselves.   —V. S. NAIPAUL

To be good is noble, but to teach others how to be good is nobler—and less trouble.   —MARK TWAIN

What is good, you ask.
To be brave is good.

—FRIEDRICH NIETZSCHE

Sin lies only in hurting others unnecessarily. All other "sins" are invented nonsense.   —ROBERT A. HEINLEIN

When you go out to seek revenge, dig two graves.
          —CHINESE PROVERB

The moral high ground ... as in most things human, was wreathed in fog. —ARTHUR MILLER

Go to work, and above all co-operate and don't hold back on one another or try to gain at the expense of another. Any success in such lopsidedness will be increasingly short-lived. These are the synergetic rules that evolution is employing and trying to make clear to us. They are not man-made laws. They are the infinitely accommodative laws of the intellectual integrity governing universe. —R. BUCKMINSTER FULLER

Far from idleness being the root of all evil, it is rather the only true good. —SØREN KIERKEGAARD

Waste no more time arguing what a good man should be. Be one. —MARCUS AURELIUS

On the whole, human beings want to be good, but not too good, and not quite all the time.
—GEORGE ORWELL

I think a man's duty is to find out where the truth is, or if he cannot, at least to take the best possible human doctrine and the hardest to disprove, and to ride on this like a raft over the waters of life. —PLATO

Conscientious people are apt to see their duty in that which is the most painful course.

—GEORGE ELIOT, *The Mill on the Floss*

You've got to have something to eat and a little love in your life before you can hold still for any damn body's sermon on how to behave. —BILLIE HOLIDAY

If I exorcise my devils, well, my angels may leave too.

—TOM WAITS, "Please Call Me, Baby"

There is no moral obligation to believe the unbelievable any more than there is a moral obligation to do what is undoable. —CARL VAN DOREN

Philosophers and theologians have yet to learn that a physical fact is as sacred as a moral principle.

—JEAN LOUIS RODOLPHE AGASSIZ

He judges not as the judge judges, but as the sun falling around a helpless thing. —WALT WHITMAN

The needle of our conscience is as good a compass as any.

—RUTH WOLFF

It is almost impossible systematically to constitute a nat-ural moral law. Nature has no principles. She furnishes us with no reason to believe that human life is to be respected. Nature, in her indifference, makes no distinction between good and evil.

—ANATOLE FRANCE, *The Revolt of the Angels*

The good die young. They do this because they see it's no use living if you've got to be good.   —JOHN BARRYMORE

Grub first, then morality.

—BERTOLT BRECHT, *The Threepenny Opera*

Morality is simply the attitude we adopt toward people we personally dislike.

—OSCAR WILDE, *An Ideal Husband*

> *Moral indignation is jealousy with a halo.*
>
> —H. G. WELLS, *The Wife of Sir Isaac Harman*

A man's ethical behavior should be based effectually on sympathy, education, and social ties; no religious basis is necessary. Man would indeed be in a poor way if he had to be restrained by fear of punishment and hope of reward after death.   —ALBERT EINSTEIN

There is only one good, namely, knowledge; and one
evil, namely, ignorance.   —SOCRATES

Yet no matter how evil your enemy is, the crucial thing
is that he is human; and although incapable of loving
another like ourselves, we nonetheless know that evil
takes root when one man starts to think that he is better
than another.   —JOSEPH BRODSKY

The belief in a single truth and in being the possessor
thereof is the root cause of all evil in the world.
                                       —MAX BORN

Boredom is a root of all evil.   —SØREN KIERKEGAARD

What is hell? I maintain that it is the suffering of being
unable to love.
        —FYODOR DOSTOYEVSKY, *The Brothers Karamazov*

Hell is just—other people.
                        —JEAN-PAUL SARTRE, *No Exit*

Whatever the future may have in store for us, one thing
is certain—this new revolution in human thought will
never go backward. When a great truth once gets abroad
in the world, no power on earth can imprison it, or pre-

scribe its limits, or suppress it. It is bound to go on till it becomes the thought of the world.

—FREDERICK DOUGLASS

Sometimes, I feel discriminated against, but it does not make me angry. It merely astonishes me. How *can* any deny themselves the pleasure of my company? It is beyond me.

—ZORA NEALE HURSTON

The meek shall inherit the earth, but not the mineral rights.

—J. PAUL GETTY (attributed)

If there is no great glorious end to all this, if nothing we do matters, then all that matters is what we do.

—JOSS WHEDON, *Angel*, "Epiphany"

The only way I can pay back for what fate and society have handed me is to try, in minor totally useless ways, to make an angry sound against injustice.

—MARTHA GELLHORN

When a stupid man is doing something he is ashamed of, he always declares that it is his duty.

—GEORGE BERNARD SHAW, *Caesar and Cleopatra*

The real definition of loneliness [is] to live without social responsibility.

—NADINE GORDIMER, *Burger's Daughter*

We did our duty as human beings: helping people in need.
—Miep Gies, who along with Johannes Kleiman,
Victor Kugler, and Elisabeth Voskuijl, risked
their lives to hide Anne Frank and her
family from the Nazis in Amsterdam

People everywhere enjoy believing things that they know are not true. It spares them the ordeal of thinking for themselves and taking responsibility for what they know.   —Brooks Atkinson

Microbiology and meteorology now explain what only a few centuries ago was considered sufficient cause to burn women to death.   —Carl Sagan

There are no heroes in this war. . . . All the heroes are dead. And the real heroes are the parents.
—Ernest Hemingway

Take me to the driest county in the most conservative state, and in two hours this determined hedonist will find you all the drugs, whores, and booze you'll need to pass an eventful weekend.   —Dan Savage

You can resolve to live your life with integrity. Let your credo be this: Let the lie come into the world, let it even triumph. But not through me.
—Aleksandr Solzhenitsyn

I used to be Snow White, but I drifted.
—MAE WEST, *I'm No Angel*

Nothing is more unpleasant than a virtuous person with a mean mind. —WALTER BAGEHOT

What men call social virtues, good fellowship, is commonly but the virtue of pigs in a litter, which lie close together to keep each other warm.
—HENRY DAVID THOREAU

Though I obviously have no proof of this, the one aspect of life that seems clear to me is that good people do whatever they believe is the right thing to do. Being virtuous is hard, not easy. The idea of doing good things simply because you're good seems like a zero-sum game; I'm not even sure those actions would still qualify as "good," since they'd merely be a function of normal behavior. —CHUCK KLOSTERMAN

A man is basically as faithful as his options.
—CHRIS ROCK

True character arises from a deeper well than religion. It is the internalization of moral principles of a society, augmented by those tenets personally chosen by the individual, strong enough to endure through trials of solitude and adversity. The principles are fitted together into what we call integrity, literally the integrated self, wherein personal decisions feel good and true. Character is in turn the enduring source of virtue. It stands by itself and excites admiration in others.   —E. O. WILSON

Mystery

Something unknown is doing we don't know what.
　　　　　　　　　　　　　　—Sir Arthur Eddington

Penetrating so many secrets, we cease to believe in the Unknowable. But there it sits, nevertheless, calmly licking its chops. 　　　　　　　　　　　—H. L. Mencken

There will come a time when our descendants will be amazed that we did not know things that are so plain to them. . . . Many discoveries are reserved for ages still to come, when memory of us will have been effaced. Our universe is a sorry little affair unless it has in it something for every age to investigate. . . . Nature does not reveal her mysteries once and for all. 　　　—Seneca

Life has unfathomable secrets. Human knowledge will be erased from the archives of the world before we possess the last word that the Gnat has to say to us.
　　　　　　　　　　　　　　—Jean Henri Fabré

As the Greeks sensibly believed, should you get to know yourself, you will have penetrated as much of the human mystery as anyone need ever know. —GORE VIDAL

Science has "explained" nothing; the more we know, the more fantastic the world becomes and the profounder the surrounding darkness. —ALDOUS HUXLEY

I have a policy about that word "soul." It is strictly prohibited except in cases of conversations having to do with okra recipes or Marvin Gaye. —SARAH VOWELL

Not *how* the world is, is the mystical, but *that* it is. —LUDWIG WITTGENSTEIN

Unseen, in the background, Fate was quietly slipping the lead into the boxing-glove.

—P. G. WODEHOUSE, *Very Good, Jeeves*

The whole problem can be stated quite simply by asking, "Is there a meaning to music?" My answer would be, "Yes." And "Can you state in so many words what the meaning is?" My answer to that would be, "No." Therein lies the difficulty. —AARON COPLAND

Somewhere, something incredible is waiting to be known.
> —*Newsweek* reporters DAVID GELMAN, SHARON
> BEGLEY, DEWEY GRAM, and EVERT CLARK

When we have found all the mysteries and lost all the meaning, we will be alone, on an empty shore.
> —TOM STOPPARD, *Arcadia*

It is not peace we seek but meaning.
> —LAWRENCE DURRELL, "The Reckoning"

I can live with doubt and uncertainty. . . . It's much more interesting to live not knowing than to have answers which might be wrong.   —RICHARD P. FEYNMAN

The true mystery of the world is the visible, not the invisible.   —OSCAR WILDE, *The Picture of Dorian Gray*

All religions will pass, but this will remain: simply sitting in a chair and looking into the distance.
> —VASILY ROZANOV

To allow mystery, which is to say to yourself, "There could be more, there could be things we don't understand," is not to damn knowledge. It is to take a wider view. It is to permit yourself to an extraordinary free-

dom: someone else does not have to be wrong in order
for you to be right. —BARRY LOPEZ

The world strikes human beings as something to be figured out, and comes with no solution.
—JENNIFER MICHAEL HECHT

Enough for me the mystery of the eternity of life, and
the inkling of the marvelous structure of reality, together
with the single-hearted endeavour to comprehend a portion, be it ever so tiny, of the reason that manifests itself
in nature. —ALBERT EINSTEIN

I find enough mystery in mathematics to satisfy my spiritual needs. I think, for example, that pi is mysterious
enough (don't get me started!) without having to worry
about God. Or if pi isn't enough, how about fractals? or
quantum mechanics? —TOM LEHRER

It is better to ask some of the questions than to know all
the answers. —JAMES THURBER

The Cosmos is all that is or was or ever will be. Our fee-
blest contemplations of the Cosmos stir us—there is a tin-
gling in the spine, a catch in the voice, a faint sensation, as
if a distant memory, of falling from a height. We know we
are approaching the greatest of mysteries. —CARL SAGAN

The theory of probability is the only mathematical tool available to help map the unknown and the uncontrollable. It is fortunate that this tool, while tricky, is extraordinarily powerful and convenient.

—BENOIT MANDELBROT

There is a theory which states that if ever anyone discovers exactly what the Universe is for and why it is here, it will instantly disappear and be replaced by something even more bizarre and inexplicable. There is another theory which states that this has already happened.

—DOUGLAS ADAMS, *The Restaurant at the End of the Universe*

The shamans are forever yakking about their snake-oil "miracles." I prefer the Real McCoy—a pregnant woman.

—ROBERT HEINLEIN, *Time Enough for Love*

Human beings . . . are far too prone to generalize from one instance. The technical word for this, interestingly enough, is superstition. —FRANCIS CRICK

We carry with us the wonders we seek without us.

—SIR THOMAS BROWNE

There is only Man, and it's he who makes miracles.

—LORRAINE HANSBERRY, *A Raisin in the Sun*

> *The good psychic would pick up
> the phone before it rang.*
>
> —ELLEN DEGENERES

It is related that Sakyamuni [the historical Buddha] once dismissed as of small consequence a feat of levitation on the part of a disciple, and cried out in pity for a yogin by the river who had spent twenty years of his human existence learning to walk on water, when the ferryman might have taken him across for a small coin.

—PETER MATTHIESSEN

Witchcraft to the ignorant . . . Simple science to the learned.

—LEIGH BRACKETT, "The Sorcerer of Rhiannon"

Nature

I have made mysterious Nature my religion. . . . To feel the supreme and moving beauty of the spectacle to which Nature invites her ephemeral guests! . . . that is what I call prayer.　　　　　　　　—Claude Debussy

If we surrendered to earth's intelligence we could rise up rooted, like trees.

—Rainer Maria Rilke,
"How Surely Gravity's Law . . ."

When I get sick of what men do, I have only to walk a few steps in another direction to see what spiders do. Or what the weather does. This sustains me very well indeed and I have no complaints.　　　　　—E. B. White

There is nothing useless in nature; not even uselessness.
　　　　　　　　　　　　—Michel de Montaigne

I don't like using the word environment. I don't like the word nature. I don't like using them because they make it seem as though we're not nature. Anything we do to the rest of the world we're doing to ourselves.

—W. S. MERWIN

There is no reason to be less moved by nature around us simply because it's revealed to have more layers of complexity than we first observed.   —ROBERT SAPOLSKY

The Amen! of Nature is always a flower.

—OLIVER WENDELL HOLMES, JR.

No matter how sophisticated you may be, a large granite mountain cannot be denied—it speaks in silence to the very core of your being.   —ANSEL ADAMS

Why in any case, this glorification of man? How about lions and tigers? They destroy fewer animals or human lives than we do, and they are much more beautiful than we are. How about ants? They manage the Corporate State much better than any Fascist. Would not a world of nightingales and larks and deer be better than our human world of cruelty and injustice and war? The believers in Cosmic Purpose make much of our supposed intelligence, but their writings make one doubt it. If I were granted omnipotence, and millions of years to experiment in, I should not think Man much to boast of as the final result of all my efforts.   —BERTRAND RUSSELL

Nature gives no permission of entry, no deed to self. Nature's silence assures us that all creatures are born equally into the fellowship of life.   —KENNETH L. PATTON

I think one could say that a certain modesty toward understanding nature is a precondition to the continued pursuit of science.

—SUBRAHMANYAN CHANDRASEKHAR

It was one of those still evenings you get in the summer, when you can hear a snail clear its throat a mile away.

—P. G. WODEHOUSE, "Jeeves Takes Charge"

The sun, with all those planets revolving around it and dependent on it, can still ripen a bunch of grapes as if it had nothing else in the universe to do.

—GALILEO GALILEI

Nature is not our enemy, to be raped and conquered. Nature is ourselves, to be cherished and explored.

—TERENCE MCKENNA

The scientific equations we seek are the poetry of nature.
—CHEN NING YANG

All knowledge is interesting to a wise man, and the knowledge of nature is interesting to all men.
—MATTHEW ARNOLD

An age builds up cities: an hour destroys them. In a moment the ashes are made, but a forest is a long time growing.
—SENECA

The planting of trees is the least self-centered of all that we can do. It is a purer act of faith than the procreation of children.
—THORNTON WILDER

In Nature there are neither rewards nor punishments—there are consequences.

—ROBERT G. INGERSOLL

I do not believe Nature has a heart; and I suspect that, like many another beauty, she has been credited with a heart because of her face.
—FRANCIS THOMPSON

I once had a sparrow alight upon my shoulder for a moment, while I was hoeing a village garden, and I felt that I was more distinguished by that circumstance than I should have been by any epaulet I could have worn.
—HENRY DAVID THOREAU

Laws of Nature are human inventions, like ghosts.
—ROBERT M. PIRSIG, *Zen and the
Art of Motorcycle Maintenance*

Nature teaches more than she preaches. There are no sermons in stones. It is easier to get a spark out of a stone than a moral. Even when it contains a fossil, it teaches history rather than morals.   —JOHN BURROUGHS

The clearest way into the Universe is through a forest wilderness.   —JOHN MUIR

[For] my church, I put a capital N on Nature and go there. . . . You spell God with a G, don't you? . . . I spell Nature with an N, capital.   —FRANK LLOYD WRIGHT

The violets in the mountains have broken the rocks.
—TENNESSEE WILLIAMS, *Camino Real*

Though I do not believe in the order of things, still the sticky little leaves that come out in the spring are dear to me, the blue sky is dear to me, some people are dear to me, whom one loves sometimes, would you believe it, without even knowing why; some human deeds are dear to me, which one has perhaps long ceased believing in, but still honors with one's heart, out of old habit.

—FYODOR DOSTOYEVSKY, *The Brothers Karamazov*

The temple bell stops but I still hear the sound coming out of the flowers.
    —MATSUO BASHŌ

Planet Earth

Brute force crushes many plants. Yet the plants rise again. The Pyramids will not last a moment compared with the daisy. And before Buddha or Jesus spoke the nightingale sang, and long after the words of Jesus and Buddha are gone into oblivion the nightingale still will sing. Because it is neither preaching nor teaching nor commanding nor urging. It is just singing. And in the beginning was not a Word, but a chirrup.
—D. H. Lawrence

I left Earth three times and found no other place to go. Please take care of Spaceship Earth.
—Wally Schirra, American Mercury, Gemini, and Apollo astronaut

Somehow the wondrous promise of the earth is that there are things beautiful in it, things wondrous and alluring, and by virtue of your trade you want to understand them.
—Mitchell Feigenbaum

How vast those Orbs must be, and how inconsiderable this Earth, the Theatre upon which all our mighty Designs, all our Navigations, and all our Wars are transacted, is when compared to them. A very fit consideration, and matter of Reflection, for those Kings and Princes who sacrifice the Lives of so many People, only to flatter their Ambition in being Masters of some pitiful corner of this small Spot.   —CHRISTIAAN HUYGENS

We are living on this planet as if we have another one to go to.   —TERRI SWEARINGEN

Sitting quietly, doing nothing, spring comes, and the grass grows by itself.

—ZEN SAYING

The goal of life is living in agreement with nature.   —ZENO OF CITIUM

There is not a sprig of grass that shoots uninteresting to me.   —THOMAS JEFFERSON

Some people are always grumbling that roses have thorns. I am thankful that thorns have roses.

—ALPHONSE KARR

How inappropriate to call this planet Earth when clearly it is Ocean. —ARTHUR C. CLARKE

I would vote for Bach, all of Bach, streamed out into space, over and over again. We would be bragging, of course, but it is surely excusable to put the best possible face on at the beginning of such an acquaintance. We can tell the harder truths later. —LEWIS THOMAS

The most beautiful (the only beautiful) (beautiful is an inadequate and temporizing improvisation) thing in the world is, of course, the world itself. This is so not only logically but categorically. —WALLACE STEVENS

To consider the Earth the only populated world in infinite space is as absurd as to assert that in an entire field sown with millet only one grain will grow. —METRODORUS OF CHIOS

There is something in living close to the great elemental forces of nature that causes people to rise above small annoyances and discomforts. —LAURA INGALLS WILDER

The Earth is a very small stage in a vast cosmic arena. . . . Our posturings, our imagined self-importance, the delusion that we have some privileged position in the Universe, are challenged by this point of pale light. Our planet is a lonely speck in the great enveloping cosmic dark. In our obscurity, in all this vastness, there is no hint that help will come from elsewhere to save us from ourselves. —CARL SAGAN

It isn't necessary that you leave home. Sit at your desk and listen. Don't even listen, just wait. Don't wait, be still and alone. The whole world will offer itself to you to be unmasked, it can do no other, it will writhe before you in ecstasy. —FRANZ KAFKA

The notion of saving the planet has nothing to do with intellectual honesty or science. The fact is that the planet was here long before us and will be here long after us. The planet is running fine. What people are talking about is saving themselves and saving their middle-class lifestyles and saving their cash flow. —LYNN MARGULIS

The world isn't waiting for you to see it; rather, it is waiting to be built by you and others. —WALTER MOSLEY

If you could see the earth illuminated when you were in a place as dark as night, it would look to you more splendid than the moon. —GALILEO GALILEI

In our world, complexity flourishes, and those looking to science for a general understanding of nature's habits will be better served by the laws of chaos.

—JAMES GLEICK

The human mind delights in finding pattern—so much so that we often mistake coincidence or forced analogy for profound meaning. No other habit of thought lies so deeply within the soul of a small creature trying to make sense of a complex world not constructed for it.

—STEPHEN JAY GOULD

You say the real, the world as it is. But it is not! It becomes. It moves, it changes. . . . The world, the real is not an object. It is a process.   —JOHN CAGE

One assumes that the world simply is and is and is but it isn't, it is like music that we hear a moment at a time and put together in our heads. But this music, unlike other music, cannot be performed again.

—RUSSELL HOBAN, *Pilgermann*

The motto I have penned on my knuckles is that this is the best world we have—because it's the only world we have. It's the simplest math ever. However many terrible, rankling, peeve-inducing things may occur, there are always libraries. And rain-falling-on-sea. And the moon. And love. There is always something to look back on, with satisfaction, or forward to, with joy. There is always a moment where you boggle at the world—at yourself—at the whole, unlikely, precarious business of being alive—and then start laughing.

—CAITLIN MORAN

> In the fight between you and the world, back the world.
>
> —FRANZ KAFKA

The world—whatever we might think when terrified by its vastness and our own impotence, or embittered by its indifference to individual suffering, of people, animals, and perhaps even plants, for why are we so sure that plants feel no pain; whatever we might think of its expanses pierced by the rays of stars surrounded by planets we've just begun to discover, planets already dead? still dead? we just don't know; whatever we might think of this measureless theater to which we've got reserved tickets, but tickets whose lifespan is laughably short, bounded as it is by two arbitrary dates; whatever else we might think of this world—it is astonishing.

—WISŁAWA SZYMBORSKA

Is not the whole world a vast house of assignation to which the filing system has been lost? —QUENTIN CRISP

The world is like a ride in an amusement park. And when you choose to go on it you think it's real because that's how powerful our minds are. And the ride goes up and down and round and round. It has thrills and chills and it's very brightly colored and it's very loud and it's fun, for a while. Some people have been on the ride for a long time and they begin to question: "Is this real, or is this just a ride?" And other people have remembered, and they come back to us, they say, "Hey, don't worry, don't be afraid, ever, because this is just a ride." And we kill those people. —BILL HICKS

A man sets out to draw the world. As the years go by, he peoples a space with images of provinces, kingdoms, mountains, bays, ships, islands, fishes, rooms, instruments, stars, horses, and individuals. A short time before he dies, he discovers that the patient labyrinth of lines traces the lineaments of his own face.

—JORGE LUIS BORGES

Relationships

It is in the shelter of each other that the people live.
—Irish proverb

There are things so deeply personal that they can only be revealed to strangers. —Richard Rodriguez

Happiness does not await us all. One needn't be a prophet to say that there will be more grief and pain than serenity and money. That is why we must hang on to one another. —Anton Chekhov

Of all the means which are procured by wisdom to ensure happiness throughout the whole of life, by far the most important is the acquisition of friends. —Epicurus

Blood may be thicker than water, but junior high school friendships are thicker than anything.
—Stephen Jay Gould, in a letter to his childhood friend Richard Milner

When you begin to see that your enemy is suffering, that is the beginning of insight. When you see in yourself the wish that the other person stop suffering, that is a sign of real love. —THICH NHAT HANH

No self is of itself alone. It has a long chain of intellectual ancestors. The "I" is chained to ancestry by many factors. . . . This is not mere allegory, but an eternal memory. —ERWIN SCHRÖDINGER

You must have four children. One for Mother, one for Father, one for Accidents, one for Increase.
—WINSTON CHURCHILL, in a letter to his wife, Clementine

One must say Yes to life, and embrace it wherever it is found—and it is found in terrible places. . . . For nothing is fixed, forever and forever, it is not fixed; the earth is always shifting, the light is always changing, the sea does not cease to grind down rock. Generations do not cease to be born, and we are responsible to them because we are the only witnesses they have. The sea rises, the light fails, lovers cling to each other and children cling to us. The moment we cease to hold each other, the moment we break faith with one another, the sea engulfs us and the light goes out. —JAMES BALDWIN

I think faith in each other is much harder than faith in God or faith in crystals.   —STEPHEN FRY

If you have to ask someone to change, to tell you they love you, to bring wine to dinner, to call you when they land, you can't afford to be with them.

—SLOANE CROSLEY

They create you. From nothing. Miracle? They do those every day. No big deal. They are not worshiped. They would give their life without the promise of heaven. They teach you everything they know yet they are not declared prophets. And you only have one.

—RICKY GERVAIS, on mothers

We're born alone, we live alone, we die alone. Only through our love and friendship can we create the illusion for the moment that we're not alone.

—ORSON WELLES, *Someone to Love*

If you want to know who your friends are, get yourself a jail sentence.   —CHARLES BUKOWSKI

Every beetle is a gazelle in the eyes of its mother.

—MOROCCAN PROVERB

We are alone, absolutely alone on this chance planet: and, amid all the forms of life that surround us, not one, excepting the dog, has made an alliance with us.

—MAURICE MAETERLINCK

If you want your children to turn out well, spend twice as much time with them as you think you should and half the amount of money.　　　　—ESTHER SELSDON

The true teacher defends his pupils against his own personal influence. He inspires self-distrust. He guides their eyes from himself to the spirit that quickens him. He will have no disciple.　　　　—AMOS BRONSON ALCOTT

A friend is a person with whom I may be sincere. Before him, I may think aloud.　　　　—RALPH WALDO EMERSON

Each friend represents a world in us, a world possibly not born until they arrive, and it is only by this meeting that a new world is born.　　　　—ANAÏS NIN

Before you eat or drink anything, consider carefully who you eat or drink with rather than what you eat or drink; not eating with a friend is the life of a lion or a wolf.

—EPICURUS

When you die, you are grieved by all the atoms of which you were composed. . . . With your death they do not die. Instead, they part ways, moving off in their separate directions, mourning the loss of a special time they shared together, haunted by the feeling that they were once playing parts in something larger than themselves, something that had its own life, something they can hardly put a finger on.

—David Eagleman, "Ineffable"

You can learn many things from children. How much patience you have, for instance.   —Franklin P. Jones

Not I but the world says it:
All is one.

—HERACLITUS

Some claim evolution is just a theory. As if it were merely an opinion. The theory of evolution, like the theory of gravity, is a scientific fact. Evolution really happened. Accepting our kinship with all life on Earth is not only solid science. In my view, it's also a soaring spiritual experience.   —Neil deGrasse Tyson

If we were to wipe out insects alone on this planet, the rest of life and humanity with it would mostly disappear from the land. Within a few months.   —E. O. Wilson

Our emancipation from the animal kingdom must be regarded as a freak of nature. The story of creation favours man and has been passed down and elaborated by the one faculty particular to us—language.

—RALPH STEADMAN

The eyes of fear want you to put bigger locks on your doors, buy guns, close yourself off. The eyes of love instead see all of us as one. —BILL HICKS

Mother's love is bliss, is peace, it need not be acquired, it need not be deserved. —ERICH FROMM

Your body is just one in a mass of cuddly humanity. Become an internationalist and learn to respect all life. Make war on machines. And in particular the sterile machines of corporate death and the robots that guard them. The duty of a revolutionary is to make love and that means staying alive and free.

—ABBIE HOFFMAN

Everything is both simpler than we can imagine and more entangled than we can conceive.

—JOHANN WOLFGANG VON GOETHE

I think that everything in life comes down to, essentially, self and not self. . . . The more [you experience] a more permeable relation to other people and other things, the more naturally that sense of wonder comes.

—David Wilson

When we speak about nature we must not forget that we are part of it. We ought to view ourselves with the same curiosity and openness with which we study a tree, the sky or a thought, because we too are linked to the entire universe. —Henri Matisse

The air in a man's lungs contains 10,000,000,000,000, 000,000,000 atoms, so that sooner or later every one of us breathes an atom that has been breathed before by anyone you can think of who has ever lived—Michelangelo or George Washington or Moses.

—Jacob Bronowski

He that will have his son have a respect for him and his orders, must himself have a great reverence for his son.

—John Locke

Let there be such oneness between us that when one cries, the other tastes salt. —Anonymous proverb

In the stillness, in the great peace that came over me, I heard the heart of the world beat. I know what the cure is: it is to give up, to relinquish, to surrender, so that our

little hearts may beat in unison with the great heart of
the world. —HENRY MILLER

We'd like him to know where he comes from and we'd
like him to reject the same religious tenets we rejected.
—DANIEL HANDLER, on raising his child as an
"observant but not particularly religious Jew"

To feel the love of people whom we know is fire that
feeds our life. But to feel the affection that comes from
those whom we do not know . . . that is something still
greater and more beautiful because it widens out the
boundaries of our being and unites all living things.
—PABLO NERUDA

Science

I love science, and it pains me to think that so many are terrified of the subject or feel that choosing science means you cannot also choose compassion, or the arts, or be awed by nature. Science is not meant to cure us of mystery, but to reinvent and reinvigorate it.

—Robert Sapolsky

Science kills credulity and superstition, but to the well-balanced mind it enhances the feeling of wonder, of veneration, and of kinship which we feel in the presence of the miraculous universe.　　　　　—John Burroughs

That's the good thing about science: it's true whether or not you believe in it.
That's why it works.

—NEIL DEGRASSE TYSON

We've got to get past this idea that science is a thing. It isn't a thing like religion is a thing or a political party is a thing. . . . But science is just a method, a way of answering questions. It's a verb not a noun.

—MICHAEL SHERMER

We can no longer argue that, for instance, the beautiful hinge of a bivalve shell must have been made by an intelligent being, like the hinge of a door by man. There seems to be no more design in the variability of organic beings, and in the action of natural selection, than in the course which the wind blows. —CHARLES DARWIN

If you want to save your child from polio, you can pray or you can inoculate. . . . Choose science.

—CARL SAGAN

What has philosophy got to do with measuring anything? It's the mathematicians you have to trust, and they measure the skies like we measure a field.

—GALILEO GALILEI

Knowledge—it excites prejudices to call it science—is advancing as irresistibly, as majestically, as remorselessly as the ocean moves in upon the shore.

—OLIVER WENDELL HOLMES, SR.

The miracle of the appropriateness of the language of mathematics for the formulation of the laws of physics is a wonderful gift which we neither understand nor deserve. —Eugene Wigner

Science cannot be stopped. Man will gather knowledge no matter what the consequences—and we cannot predict what they will be. . . . But I know also that still more interesting discoveries will be made that I have not the imagination to describe—and I am awaiting them, full of curiosity and enthusiasm. —Linus Pauling

If scientists don't play God, who else is going to? —James D. Watson

My ambition is to live to see all of physics reduced to a formula so elegant and simple that it will fit easily on the front of a T-shirt. —Leon Lederman

Whoever wins to a great scientific truth will find a poet before him in the quest. —Frederic Wood-Jones

All is number. —Pythagoras

All science is either physics or stamp collecting. —Ernest Rutherford

You have only to wish it and you can have a world without hunger, disease, cancer and toil—anything you wish,

wish anything and it can be done. Or else we can exterminate ourselves . . . at present we are on the road to extermination.   —ALBERT SZENT-GYÖRGYI

The science of life is a superb and dazzlingly lighted hall which may be reached only by passing through a long and ghastly kitchen.   —CLAUDE BERNARD

There is no great invention, from fire to flying, which has not been hailed as an insult to some god.
                    —J. B. S. HALDANE

If [science] tends to thicken the crust of ice on which, as it were, we are skating, it is all right. If it tries to find, or professes to have found, the solid ground at the bottom of the water, it is all wrong. Our business is with the thickening of this crust by extending our knowledge downward from above, as ice gets thicker while the frost lasts; we should not try to freeze upwards from the bottom.   —SAMUEL BUTLER

It is often stated that of all the theories proposed in this century, the silliest is quantum theory. In fact, some say that the only thing that quantum theory has going for it is that it is unquestionably correct.   —MICHIO KAKU

[Darwin's theory of evolution by natural selection] was a concept of such stunning simplicity, but it gave rise, naturally, to all of the infinite and baffling complexity of life. The awe it inspired in me made the awe that people talk about in respect of religious experience seem, frankly, silly beside it. I'd take the awe of understanding over the awe of ignorance any day.

—Douglas Adams, *The Salmon of Doubt*

There is no democracy in physics. We can't say that some second-rate guy has as much right to opinion as Fermi.

—Luis Walter Alvarez

Science is imagination in the service of the verifiable truth.

—GERALD EDELMAN

In most sciences one generation tears down what another has built and what one has established another one undoes. In mathematics alone each generation adds a new story to the old structure.　　—Hermann Hankel

If people do not believe that mathematics is simple, it is only because they do not realize how complicated life is.

—John von Neumann

One cannot escape the feeling that these mathematical formulas have an independent existence and an intelligence of their own, that they are wiser than we are, wiser even than their discoverers, that we get more out of them than was originally put into them.

—Heinrich Hertz

Magnetism is one of the Six Fundamental Forces of the Universe, with the other five being Gravity, Duct Tape, Whining, Remote Control, and The Force That Pulls Dogs Toward the Groins of Strangers. —Dave Barry

Clarke's First Law: When a distinguished but elderly scientist states that something is possible he is almost certainly right. When he states that something is impossible, he is very probably wrong. —Arthur C. Clarke

It is a mathematical fact that the casting of this pebble from my hand alters the center of gravity in the universe. —Thomas Carlyle

Science is a differential equation. Religion is a boundary condition. —Alan Turing

Human beings are so destructive. I sometimes think we're a kind of plague, that will scrub the earth clean. We destroy things so well that I sometimes think, maybe that's our function. Maybe every few eons, some animal comes along that kills off the rest of the world, clears the decks, and lets evolution proceed to its next phase.

—MICHAEL CRICHTON, *The Lost World*

There is no better, there is no more open door by which you can enter into the study of natural philosophy, than by considering the physical phenomena of a candle.

—MICHAEL FARADAY

Folks, it's time to evolve. That's why we're troubled. You know why our institutions are failing us, the church, the state, everything's failing? It's because, um—they're no longer relevant. We're supposed to keep evolving. Evolution did not end with us growing opposable thumbs. You do know that, right?   —BILL HICKS

One person out of one will die.   —WARREN MILLER

It is best to read the weather forecast before we pray for rain.   —MARK TWAIN

But evolution is only a theory! Which is true. I mean, it is only a theory, it's good that they say that. I think, it gives you hope, doesn't it? That maybe they feel the same way about the theory of gravity, and they might just float the fuck away.   —TIM MINCHIN

Religions die when they are proved to be true. Science is the record of dead religions. —Oscar Wilde

Stay in college, get the knowledge, stay there until you are through. If they can make penicillin out of moldy bread, they can sure make something of you.
—Muhammad Ali

Assessing existence while failing to embrace the insights of modern physics would be like wrestling in the dark with an unknown opponent. By deepening our understanding of the true nature of physical reality, we profoundly reconfigure our sense of ourselves and our experience of the universe. —Brian Greene

Nothing exists except atoms and empty space; everything else is opinion.

—DEMOCRITUS OF ABDERA

Still, if history and science have taught us anything, it is that passion and desire are not the same as truth. The human mind evolved to believe in the gods. It did not evolve to believe in biology. Acceptance of the supernatural conveyed a great advantage throughout prehistory when the brain was evolving. Thus it is in sharp contrast to biology, which was developed as a product of the modern age and is not underwritten by genetic algorithms. The uncomfortable truth is that the two beliefs are not factually compatible. As a result those who hunger for both intellectual and religious truth will never acquire both in full measure.   —E. O. WILSON

Of God, the Devil and Darwin, we have really good scientific evidence for the existence of only Darwin.
                                                      —NIALL SHANKS

There is a philosophy that says that if something is unobservable—unobservable in principle—it is not part of science. If there is no way to falsify or confirm a hypothesis, it belongs to the realm of metaphysical speculation, together with astrology and spiritualism. By that standard, most of the universe has no scientific reality—it's just a figment of our imaginations. But it is hard to dismiss most of the universe as nonsense.   —LEONARD SUSSKIND

The notion of order in the universe became something which was essential to my psychological well-being and which I have to believe in, and which was confirmed wonderfully by chemistry and the periodic table and beauty and clarity with which the universe seemed to be put together.   —OLIVER SACKS

We are not evolution's ultimate product. There's something coming after us, and I imagine it is something wonderful. But we may never be able to comprehend it, any more than a caterpillar can comprehend turning into a butterfly. —DANNY HILLIS

When I look out of my window past my computer to the bridge over the river and trees and cows in the distance, I delight in the simple and elegant creative process that brought them all into being, and at my own tiny place within in all. —SUSAN BLACKMORE

From now on, we live in a world where man has walked on the moon. And it's not a miracle, we just decided to go. —JIM LOVELL, Apollo astronaut

Sex

It's something big and cosmic. What else do we have? There's only birth and death and the union of two people—and sex is the only one that happens to us more than once. —KATHLEEN WINSOR

If your sexual fantasies were truly of interest to others, they would no longer be fantasies. —FRAN LEBOWITZ

Moral rules ought not to be such as to make instinctive happiness impossible. —BERTRAND RUSSELL

Sex cannot be understood because nature cannot be understood. Science is a method of logical analysis of nature's operations. It has lessened human anxiety about the cosmos by demonstrating the materiality of nature's forces, and their frequent predictability. But science is always playing catch-up ball. Nature breaks its own rules whenever it wants. Science cannot avert a single thunderbolt. —CAMILLE PAGLIA

In this life, you can choose between two courses. You can either shut yourself up in a country house and stare into tanks, or you can be a dasher with the sex. You can't do both. —P. G. WODEHOUSE, *Right Ho, Jeeves*

The hen is only the egg's way of making another egg.
—SAMUEL BUTLER

[Man] has imagined a heaven, and has left entirely out of it the supremest of all his delights, the one ecstasy that stands first and foremost in the heart of every individual of his race . . . sexual intercourse! It is as if a lost and perishing person in a roasting desert should be told by a rescuer he might choose and have all longed-for things but one, and he should elect to leave out water!
—MARK TWAIN

In America an obsession. In other parts of the world a fact. —MARLENE DIETRICH, on sex

Society

Whenever you find yourself on the side of the majority, it's time to pause and reflect. —MARK TWAIN

The reason I don't worry about society is, nineteen people knocked down two buildings and killed thousands. Hundreds of people ran into those buildings to save them. I'll take those odds every fucking day.
—JON STEWART, on what he witnessed in New York City on 9/11

Religion & Govt. will both exist in greater purity, the less they are mixed together. —JAMES MADISON

Encourage free schools, and resolve that not one dollar appropriated for their support shall be appropriated to the support of any sectarian school. . . . Leave the matter of religion to the family altar, the Church, and the private schools, supported entirely by private contributions. Keep the church and state forever separate.
—ULYSSES S. GRANT

Everybody thinks that this civilization has lasted a very long time but it really does take very few grandfathers' granddaughters to take us back to the dark ages.

—GERTRUDE STEIN

Those who profess to favor freedom, and yet deprecate agitation, are men who want crops without plowing up the ground. They want rain without thunder and lightning. They want the ocean without the awful roar of its many waters. . . . Power concedes nothing without a demand. It never did and it never will. Find out just what any people will submit to, and you have found out the exact amount of injustice and wrong which will be imposed upon them.

—FREDERICK DOUGLASS

The survival of democracy depends on the ability of large numbers of people to make realistic choices in the light of adequate information.

—ALDOUS HUXLEY

People do come along and lead. And they're men—they're people. And they live and breathe, and they have fears and flaws. This country wasn't made by the guy up on the mountaintop with the stone tablet. *People* made it.

—TOMMY LEE JONES

And if the word integration means anything, this is what it means: that we, with love, shall force our brothers to see themselves as they are, to cease fleeing from reality and begin to change it. For this is your home, my friend, do not be driven from it; great men have done great things here, and will again, and we can make America what America must become. —JAMES BALDWIN

Much of what is today called "social criticism" consists of members of the upper classes denouncing the tastes of the lower classes (bawdy entertainment, fast food, plentiful consumer goods) while considering themselves egalitarians. —STEVEN PINKER

Those who can make you believe absurdities, can make you commit atrocities.

—VOLTAIRE

Peace on earth would be the end of civilization as we know it. —JOSEPH HELLER

Democracy is the recurrent suspicion that more than half of the people are right more than half of the time. It is the feeling of privacy in the voting booths, the feeling of communion in the libraries, the feeling of vitality everywhere. Democracy is the letter to the editor. Democracy is the score at the beginning of the ninth. It is an idea which hasn't been disproved yet, a song the words of which have not gone bad. It's the mustard on the hot dog and the cream in the rationed coffee.

—E. B. WHITE

Live and let live and remember this line / "Your bus'ness is your bus'ness and my bus'ness is mine."

—COLE PORTER, "Live and Let Live"

Insanity in individuals is something rare—but in groups, parties, nations, and epochs, it is the rule.

—FRIEDRICH NIETZSCHE

All the misfortunes of mankind, all the sad reverses with which history is filled, the political blunders, the miscarriage of great commanders, all this comes from want of skill in dancing.

—MOLIÈRE, *The Citizen Who Apes the Nobleman*

Civilization is a movement, not a condition; a voyage, not a harbor. —ARNOLD TOYNBEE

A community is a butcher and a doctor, a minister, a town troublemaker. A "community" is not a bunch of people united by some grievance. That's just self-righteousness—incredibly dangerous and antidemocratic. —FRAN LEBOWITZ

The only sane policy for the world is that of abolishing war. —LINUS PAULING

A country is only good, where life is a dignity, where each man has his dignity and need not scratch or kick people around, to live. —MARTHA GELLHORN

If a bullet should enter my brain, let that bullet destroy every closet door in the country.
            —HARVEY MILK, in a tape recording he made to be
                    played in the event of his assassination

What is not good for the beehive, cannot be good for the bees. —MARCUS AURELIUS

I don't know what weapons World War Three will be fought with, but World War Four will be fought with sticks and stones. —ALBERT EINSTEIN

Success and Failure

Nothing you can't spell will ever work. —WILL ROGERS

It is impossible to live without failing at something, unless you live so cautiously that you might as well have not lived at all—in which case you fail by default.
—J. K. ROWLING

Jump off the cliff and learn how to make wings on the way down.   —RAY BRADBURY

The difficult is what takes a little time; the impossible is what takes a little longer.   —FRIDTJOF NANSEN

A man with a new idea is a crank until he succeeds.
—MARK TWAIN

In writing, I've always had a lot of confidence, mixed with a dread that this confidence is entirely misplaced.
—ALICE MUNRO

We've been around long enough and have been to enough award shows to know that it is easy to lose to Phil Collins at any time. —MATT STONE

Walls turned sideways are bridges.

—ANGELA DAVIS

We are born what we are; we die what we are. Success and failure are illusions. We have the universe.
—KENNETH L. PATTON

It's only those who do nothing that make no mistakes, I suppose. —JOSEPH CONRAD, *An Outcast of the Islands*

I do want to get rich but I never want to do what there is to do to get rich. —GERTRUDE STEIN

Life is not always a matter of holding good cards, but sometimes, playing a poor hand well. —JACK LONDON

Bacteria represent the world's greatest success story. They are today and have always been the modal organisms on earth; they cannot be nuked to oblivion and will outlive us all. This time is their time, not the "age of mammals" as our textbooks chauvinistically proclaim.
—STEPHEN JAY GOULD

Please know that I am aware of the hazards. I want to do it because I want to do it.

— AMELIA EARHART, on the eve of her last flight

It is not worthy of a human being to give up.

— ALVA MYRDAL

I don't like people who have never fallen or stumbled. Their virtue is lifeless and it isn't of much value. Life hasn't revealed its beauty to them.

— BORIS PASTERNAK, *Doctor Zhivago*

Remembering that you are going to die is the best way I know to avoid the trap of thinking you have something to lose. You are already naked. There is no reason not to follow your heart.   — STEVE JOBS

It is difficult to say what is impossible. For the dream of yesterday is the hope of today and the reality of tomorrow.

— ROBERT GODDARD, father of modern rocketry, whose ideas for space travel were mocked during his lifetime but successfully formed the basis of space travel after his death

Ever tried. Ever failed. No matter. Try again. Fail again. Fail better.   — SAMUEL BECKETT, *Worstward Ho*

Not failure, but low aim, is the crime. In great attempts it is glorious even to fail.   —BRUCE LEE

I cannot afford to waste my time making money.
                —JEAN LOUIS RODOLPHE AGASSIZ (attributed)

It's all about money, not freedom, ya'll, okay? Nothing to do with fuckin' freedom. If you think you're free, try going somewhere without fucking money, okay?
                —BILL HICKS

Money frees you from doing things you dislike. Since I dislike doing nearly everything, money is handy.
                —GROUCHO MARX

Time

This web of time—the strands of which approach one another, bifurcate, intersect or ignore each other through the centuries—embrace every possibility.
    —Jorge Luis Borges, "The Garden of Forking Paths"

He who owns a veteran bur oak owns more than a tree. He owns a historical library, and a reserved seat in the theater of evolution.   —Aldo Leopold

Just because you're not a drummer, doesn't mean you don't have to keep time.   —Thelonious Monk

Only our concept of time makes it possible for us to speak of the Day of Judgment by that name; in reality it is a summary court in perpetual session.
                —Franz Kafka, *The Great Wall of China*

While we are postponing, life speeds by. Nothing . . . is ours, except time.   —Seneca

Truth is the daughter of time, not of authority.

—Francis Bacon

The future will one day be the present and will seem as unimportant as the present does now.

—W. Somerset Maugham

> *Music is the best means we have of digesting time.*
>
> —IGOR STRAVINSKY

He sees eternity less like a play with a prologue and a denouement . . . he sees eternity in men and women.

—Walt Whitman

From time to time, as we all know, a sect appears in our midst announcing that the world will very soon come to an end. Generally, by some slight confusion or miscalculation, it is the sect that comes to an end.

—G. K. Chesterton

Years are only garments, and you either wear them with style all your life, or else you go dowdy to the grave.

—Dorothy Parker

It is difficult beyond description to conceive that space can have no end; but it is more difficult to conceive an end. It is difficult beyond the power of man to conceive an eternal duration of what we call time; but it is more impossible to conceive when there shall be no time.

—THOMAS PAINE

Everyone comes from an old family. It's just my family wrote everything down.

—TILDA SWINTON, whose family lineage can be traced back to 876 CE

It doesn't seem, actually, when we look at the way people behave, that lack of time is their problem. On the contrary . . . when you look at how much time we waste, [it seems] that life is already too long—so long that we become complacent and we waste great swathes, so many hours.
—STEPHEN CAVE

Time is a great teacher, but unfortunately it kills all its pupils.
—HECTOR BERLIOZ

Time has two aspects. One is the arrow, the running river without which there is no change, no progress, or direction, or creation. And there is the circle or the cycle, without which there is chaos, meaningless succession of instants, a world without clocks or seasons or promises.
—URSULA K. LE GUIN, *The Dispossessed*

There are some things which cannot be learned quickly, and time, which is all we have, must be paid heavily for their acquiring. They are the very simplest things and, because it takes a man's life to know them, the little new that each man gets from life is very costly and the only heritage he has to leave. —ERNEST HEMINGWAY

Half our life is spent trying to find something to do with the time we have rushed through life trying to save.
—WILL ROGERS

I confess that in 1901 I said to my brother Orville that man would not fly for fifty years. Two years later we ourselves made flights. This demonstration of my impotence as a prophet gave me such a shock that ever since I have distrusted myself and avoided all predictions.
—WILBUR WRIGHT

There is no rest of life. Life is one. Without beginning, without middle, without ending. The concept: beginning middle and meaning comes from a sense of self which separates itself from what it considers to be the rest of life. But this attitude is untenable unless one insists on stopping life and bringing it to an end. That thought is in itself an attempt to stop life, for life goes on, indifferent to the deaths that are part of its no beginning, no middle, no meaning. —JOHN CAGE

I have no vision of the future. I never have. There is nothing to consider other than today. I'm saving tranquility for when I'm dead.　　　　　　　—MORRISSEY

With infinite life comes an infinite list of relatives. Grandparents never die, nor do great-grandparents, great-aunts . . . and so on, back through the generations, all alive and offering advice. Sons never escape from the shadows of their fathers. Nor do daughters of their mothers. No one ever comes into his own. . . . Such is the cost of immortality. No person is whole. No person is free.　　　　　　—ALAN LIGHTMAN, *Einstein's Dreams*

There is only one place, and that place is time.
　　　　　　　　　　　　　　　　—RUSSELL HOBAN,
　　　　　　　The Lion of Boaz-Jachin and Jachin-Boaz

Truth

Precisely because of human fallibility, extraordinary claims require extraordinary evidence. —CARL SAGAN

Plato is my friend, but truth is my greater friend.
—ARISTOTLE (used as an epigraph by Isaac Newton in his 1661 notebook in which he first began investigating the properties of gravity)

Only the madman is absolutely sure.

—ROBERT SHEA and ROBERT ANTON WILSON

If history reveals any categorical truth, it is that an insufficient taste for evidence regularly brings out the worst in us. —SAM HARRIS

I don't think in terms of "truth is beauty" or "beauty is truth." I prefer what works, not elegant so much as economical. —LISA RANDALL

The first and last thing which is required of genius is the love of truth. —JOHANN WOLFGANG VON GOETHE

Nature is a source of truth. Experience does not ever err, it is only your judgment that errs in promising itself results which are not caused by your experiments.
—LEONARDO DA VINCI

Clouds are not spheres, mountains are not cones, coastlines are not circles, and bark is not smooth, nor does lightning travel in a straight line.
—BENOIT MANDELBROT, on recognizing the complexity of the world around us

Truth is tough. It will not break, like a bubble, at a touch; nay, you may kick it about all day, like a football, and it will be round and full at evening.
—OLIVER WENDELL HOLMES, SR.

What can be asserted without proof can be dismissed without proof. —CHRISTOPHER HITCHENS

An open society such as ours is based on the recognition that our understanding of reality is inherently imperfect. Nobody is in possession of the ultimate truth.

—GEORGE SOROS

Wiener's Law of Libraries: There are no answers, only cross-references. —NORBERT WIENER

A person obsessed with ultimate truth is a person asking to be relieved of money. —ROBERT B. LAUGHLIN

See now the power of truth; the same experiment which at first glance seemed to show one thing, when more carefully examined, assures us of the contrary.

—GALILEO GALILEI

The opposite of a correct statement is a false statement. The opposite of a profound truth may well be another profound truth. —NIELS BOHR

Men occasionally stumble over the truth, but most of them pick themselves up and hurry off as if nothing had happened. —WINSTON CHURCHILL

It is the certainty that they possess the truth that makes men cruel. —ANATOLE FRANCE

With the beginning of life, comes the thirst for truth, whereas the ability to lie is gradually acquired in the process of trying to stay alive.   —GAO XINGJIAN

Lying is done with words and also with silence.

—ADRIENNE RICH

Truth is the daughter of search.   —ARABIC PROVERB

Slander is played on a tin horn, while truth steals forth like the dying song of a lute.   —JOSH BILLINGS

Nothing is too wonderful to be true, if it be consistent with the laws of nature.   —MICHAEL FARADAY

Problems that remain persistently insoluble should always be suspected as questions asked in the wrong way.   —ALAN WATTS

You possess only whatever will not be lost in a shipwreck.   —EL-GHAZALI

The greatest and noblest pleasure which men can have in this world is to discover new truths; and the next is to shake off old prejudices.   —FREDERICK THE GREAT

In physics the truth is rarely perfectly clear, and that is certainly universally the case in human affairs. Hence, what is not surrounded by uncertainty cannot be the truth. —RICHARD P. FEYNMAN

Science and philosophy cast a net of words into the sea of being, happy in the end if they draw anything out besides the net itself, with some holes in it. . . . Far be it from me to deride the imagination, poetic or dialectical; but after all it is a great advantage for a system of philosophy to be substantially true.

—GEORGE SANTAYANA

The obscure we see eventually. The completely obvious, it seems takes longer.

—EDWARD R. MURROW (attributed)

The language of truth is simple.   —EURIPIDES

Since we have explored the maze so long without result, it follows for poor human reasons, that we cannot have to explore much longer; close by must be the center, with a champagne luncheon and a piece of ornamental water. How if there were no center at all, but just one alley after another, and the whole world a labyrinth without end or issue?   —ROBERT LOUIS STEVENSON

There are two kinds of light—the glow that illumines, and the glare that obscures. —JAMES THURBER

Nothing in fine print is ever good news.
—ANDY ROONEY

Serious things cannot be understood without laughable things, nor opposites at all without opposites.
—PLATO

Speak the truth, but leave immediately after.
—SLOVENIAN PROVERB

History is a construct consequent upon the questions asked by the historian. —E. H. CARR

It might be a good idea if the various countries of the world would occasionally swap history books, just to see what other people are doing with the same set of facts.
—BILL VAUGHAN

There are no facts, only interpretations.
—FRIEDRICH NIETZSCHE

There's nothing as deceptive as an obvious fact.
—SIR ARTHUR CONAN DOYLE,
The Boscombe Valley Mystery

One doesn't discover new lands without consenting to
lose sight of the shore for a very long time.
—André Gide, *The Counterfeiters*

No pressure, no diamonds.   —Anonymous

All human beings, by nature, desire to know.
—Aristotle

If a man will begin in certainties, he shall end in doubts;
but if he will be content to begin with doubt he shall end
in certainties.   —Francis Bacon

If I look over my life, every single step of maturing for
me, every single one, has had the exact same common
denominator, and that was accepting what was true over
what I wished were true.   —Julia Sweeney

I don't know what I may seem to the world, but, as to
myself, I seem to have been only like a boy playing on
the seashore and diverting myself in now and then finding a smoother pebble or a prettier shell than ordinary,
whilst the great ocean of truth lay all undiscovered before me.   —Isaac Newton

What is to give light must endure burning.
—Viktor Frankl (attributed)

There is no good in arguing with the inevitable. The only argument available with an east wind is to put on your overcoat. —JAMES RUSSELL LOWELL

You can always try to solve a problem by proving that no solution exists. —EDWARD HENRY LORENZ

Up to the Twentieth Century, reality was everything humans could touch, smell, see, and hear. Since the initial publication of the chart of the electromagnetic spectrum, humans have learned that what they can touch, smell, see, and hear is less than one-millionth of reality. —R. BUCKMINSTER FULLER

The real tension is not between matter and spirit, or time and space, the real tension is between information and nonsense. —TERENCE MCKENNA

Science shows us that the visible world is neither matter nor spirit; the visible world is the invisible organization of energy. —HEINZ R. PAGELS

Reality is that which, when you stop believing in it, doesn't go away.

—PHILIP K. DICK

You and I do not see things as they are. We see things as we are. —HERB COHEN

There is no absolute up or down, as Aristotle taught; no absolute position in space; but the position of a body is relative to that of other bodies. Everywhere there is incessant relative change in position throughout the universe, and the observer is always at the center of things.
—GIORDANO BRUNO

You can observe a lot by watching. —YOGI BERRA

Nothing is more real than nothing.
—SAMUEL BECKETT, paraphrasing Democritus in
Malone Dies

An actually existent fly is more important than a possibly existent angel. —RALPH WALDO EMERSON

Since everything is but an apparition, perfect in being what it is, having nothing to do with good or bad, acceptance or rejection, one may well burst out in laughter.
—LONGCHENPA

Reason means truth and those who are not governed by it take the chance that someday the sunken fact will rip the bottom out of their boat.
—OLIVER WENDELL HOLMES, JR.

Everyone is entitled to his own opinion, but not his own facts.
                                    —DANIEL PATRICK MOYNIHAN

Man is impelled to invent theories to account for what happens in the world. Unfortunately, he is not quite intelligent enough, in most cases, to find correct explanations.
                                    —ALDOUS HUXLEY

Contrary to popular opinion, mathematics is about simplifying life, not complicating it.
                                    —BENOIT MANDELBROT

Freethinkers are those who are willing to use their minds without prejudice and without fearing to understand things that clash with their own customs, privileges, or beliefs. This state of mind is not common, but it is essential for right thinking; where it is absent, discussion is apt to become worse than useless.
                                    —LEO TOLSTOY

The voice of the intellect is a soft one, but it does not rest until it has gained a hearing. Ultimately, after endlessly repeated rebuffs, it succeeds. This is one of the few points in which one may be optimistic about the future of mankind, but in itself it signifies not a little.
                                    —SIGMUND FREUD

Reason is to the estimation of the *philosophe* what grace is to the Christian. Grace determines the Christian's action; reason the *philosophe's*.   —DENIS DIDEROT

Fortune but seldom interferes with the wise person; his greatest and highest interests have been, are, and will be, directed by reason throughout the course of his life.
                                                —EPICURUS

The supreme maxim in scientific philosophising is this: wherever possible, logical constructions are to be substituted for inferred entities.   —BERTRAND RUSSELL

That hardest thing to understand is why we can understand anything at all.   —ALBERT EINSTEIN

It is better to hide ignorance, but it is hard to do this when we relax over wine.   —HERACLITUS

Forgive me my nonsense as I also forgive the nonsense of those who think they talk sense.   —ROBERT FROST

If forty million people say a foolish thing, it does not become a wise one.   —W. SOMERSET MAUGHAM

Stupidity does not give way to science, technology, modernity, progress; on the contrary, it progresses right along with progress! —MILAN KUNDERA

Look into the eyes of a chicken and you will see real stupidity. It is a kind of bottomless stupidity, a fiendish stupidity. They are the most horrifying, cannibalistic, and nightmarish creatures in this world.

—WERNER HERZOG

The Universe

Everything existing in the universe is the fruit of chance.
—Democritus

This universe, which is the same for all, has not been made by any god or man, but it always has been, is, and will be an ever-living fire, kindling itself by regular measures and going out by regular measures.
—Heraclitus

The universe is remarkable, because we can understand it. That's what's remarkable.   —Janna Levin

And you know the reason I really love the stars is that we cannot hurt them. We can't bum them or melt them or make them overflow. We can't flood them or burn them up or turn them out. But we are reaching for them. We are reaching for them.
—Laurie Anderson, "Another Day in America"

Praised be the fathomless universe / For life and joy and for objects and knowledge curious.
—WALT WHITMAN, "When Lilacs Last in the Dooryard Bloom'd"

As a working hypothesis to explain the riddle of our existence, I propose that our universe is the most interesting of all possible universes, and our fate as human beings is to make it so. —FREEMAN J. DYSON

It is my supposition that the Universe is not only queerer than we imagine, it is queerer than we can imagine.
—J. B. S. HALDANE

The stars died so that you could be here today.

—LAWRENCE KRAUSS

I was reading about how countless species are being pushed toward extinction by man's destruction of forests. Sometimes I think the surest sign that intelligent life exists elsewhere in the universe is that none of it has tried to contact us. —BILL WATTERSON, *Calvin and Hobbes*

What is the universe? Is it a great 3D movie in which we are the unwilling actors? Is it a cosmic joke, a giant computer, a work of art by a Supreme Being, or simply an experiment? The problem in trying to understand the universe is that we have nothing to compare it with.

—Heinz R. Pagels

There are more things in heaven and earth, / Horatio, / Than are dreamt of in your philosophy.

—William Shakespeare, *Hamlet*

There's only one corner of the universe you can be certain of improving, and that's your own self.

—Aldous Huxley

Every grain of sand, every tip of a leaf, even an atom, contains the entire universe. Conversely, the universe can be perceived as the tip of a leaf.

—Gerhard Staguhn

My goal is simple. It is a complete understanding of the universe, why it is as it is and why it exists at all.

—Stephen Hawking

The universe is made of stories, not of atoms.

—Muriel Rukeyser, "The Speed of Darkness"

It is well to remember that the entire universe, with one trifling exception, is composed of others.

—JOHN ANDREW HOLMES

Color is the place where our brain and the universe meet.

—PAUL CÉZANNE

It is inconceivable that the whole Universe was merely created for us who live in this third-rate planet of a third-rate sun.

—ALFRED, LORD TENNYSON

If you're looking for the key to the universe, I have some bad news and some good news. The bad news is that there is no key to the universe. The good news is that it has been left unlocked.

—ANONYMOUS

The fact that we live at the bottom of a deep gravity well, on the surface of a gas covered planet going around a nuclear fireball 90 million miles away and think this to be normal is obviously some indication of how skewed our perspective tends to be.

—DOUGLAS ADAMS

The heart that breaks open can contain the whole universe.

—JOANNA ROGERS MACY

The universe is so *un*human . . . it goes its way with so little thought of man. He is but an incident, not an end. We must adjust our notions to the discovery that things are not shaped to him, but that he is shaped to them. The air was not made for his lungs, but he has lungs because there is air; the light was not created for his eye, but he has eyes because there is light. All the forces of nature are going their own way; man avails himself of them, or catches a ride as best he can.   —JOHN BURROUGHS

If it's true that our species is alone in the universe, then I'd have to say that the universe aimed rather low and settled for very little.   —GEORGE CARLIN

Human beings have a natural tendency to look for meaning and purpose out there in the universe, but we shouldn't elevate that tendency to a cosmic principle. Meaning and purpose are created by us, not lurking somewhere within the ultimate architecture of reality.
  —SEAN CARROLL

Man is a piece of the universe made alive.
  —RALPH WALDO EMERSON

If the stars are suns and the earth is the earth and there are men only upon this earth and anything can put an end to anything and any dog does anything like anybody

does it what is the difference between eternity and anything.   —GERTRUDE STEIN

The universe is full of magical things patiently waiting
for our wits to grow sharper.
                    —EDEN PHILLPOTTS, *A Shadow Passes*

Wisdom

Distance makes the mountain blue and the man great.
—ICELANDIC PROVERB

Never stay up on the barren heights of cleverness, but come down into the green valleys of silliness.
—LUDWIG WITTGENSTEIN

A man thinks that by mouthing hard words he understands hard things.
—HERMAN MELVILLE, *White-Jacket; or, The World in a Man-of-War*

The beginning of wisdom is to do away with fear.

—YOHANNES GEBREGEORGIS

I don't let my mouth say nothing my head can't stand.
—LOUIS ARMSTRONG

City wisdom became almost entirely centered on the problems of human relationships, in contrast to the wisdom of any natural tribal group, where relationships with the rest of the animate and inanimate world are still given due place. —JAMES LOVELOCK

The spread, both in width and depth, of the multifarious branches of knowledge during the last hundred odd years has confronted us with a queer dilemma. We feel clearly that we are only now beginning to acquire reliable material for welding together the sum total of all that is known into a whole; but, on the other hand, it has become next to impossible for a single mind fully to command more than a small specialized portion of it.
—ERWIN SCHRÖDINGER

There are years that ask questions and years that answer.
—ZORA NEALE HURSTON,
Their Eyes Were Watching God

The last word in ignorance is the man who says of an animal or plant, "What good is it?" If the land mechanism as a whole is good, then every part is good, whether we understand it or not. If the biota, in the course of aeons, has built something we like but do not understand, then who but a fool would discard seemingly useless parts? To keep every cog and wheel is the first precaution of intelligent tinkering.

—ALDO LEOPOLD

I suppose it is tempting, if the only tool you have is a hammer, to treat everything as if it were a nail.

—ABRAHAM MASLOW

You never understand everything. When one understands everything, one has gone crazy.

—PHILIP ANDERSON

This is education: To learn to wish that things should happen as they do. —STOIC MAXIM

What you're doing instead of your real job is your real job. —ANONYMOUS

Knowledge is proud that he has learned so much; wisdom is humble that he knows no more.

—WILLIAM COWPER

The human mind always makes progress, but it is progress in spirals. —MADAME DE STAËL

Anything worth doing is worth doing slowly.
—MAE WEST (attributed)

Silence is one of the hardest arguments to refute.
—JOSH BILLINGS

Rigid, the skeleton of habit alone upholds the human frame. —VIRGINIA WOOLF, *Mrs. Dalloway*

A genius is someone who has two great ideas.

—JACOB BRONOWSKI

If one cannot state a matter clearly enough so that even an intelligent twelve-year-old can understand it, one should remain within the cloistered walls of the university and laboratory until one gets a better grasp of one's subject matter. —MARGARET MEAD

Too much consistency is as bad for the mind as it is for the body. Consistency is contrary to nature, contrary to life. The only completely consistent people are the dead.

—ALDOUS HUXLEY

Learning acquired in youth arrests the evil of old age; and if you understand that old age has wisdom for its food, you will so conduct yourself in youth that your old age will not lack for nourishment.

—LEONARDO DA VINCI

I do not believe in a fate that falls on men however they act; but I do believe in a fate that falls on them unless they act.

—G. K. CHESTERTON

Lots of folks confuse bad management with destiny.

—FRANK "KIN" HUBBARD

You are lost the instant you know what the result will be.

—JUAN GRIS

Human history becomes more and more a race between education and catastrophe.

—H. G. WELLS

You can think as much as you like but you will invent nothing better than bread and salt.

—RUSSIAN PROVERB

We shed as we pick up, like travellers who must carry everything in their arms, and what we let fall will be picked up by those behind. The procession is very long and life is very short. We die on the march. But there is nothing outside the march so nothing can be lost to it.

—TOM STOPPARD, *Arcadia*

Wonder

Barn's burnt down—
Now
I can see the moon.

—Mizuta Masahide

There is light in shadow, and shadow in light, / And black in the blue of the sky.

—Lucy Larcom, "Blue in Black Sky"

People say there's delays on flights . . . really? New York to California in 5 hours. That used to take thirty years to do that and a bunch of you would die on the way there and have a baby. You'd be with a whole different group of people by the time you got there.   —Louis C. K.

Like Confucius of old, I am absorbed in the wonder of earth, and the life upon it, and I cannot think of heaven and the angels. I have enough for this life. If there is no other life, then this one has been enough to make it

worth being born, myself a human being. With so profound a faith in the human heart and its power to grow
toward the light, I find here reason and cause enough for
hope and confidence in the future of mankind.

—PEARL S. BUCK

The sacred is right now, you and me, whatever is happening.   —MARIE HOWE

Whoever invented the word "grace" must have seen the
wing-folding of the plover.   —ALDO LEOPOLD

We're just people stuck on this planet in the midst of the
solar system. It's incredible how much we've figured
out . . . about the places—deep space—we haven't been
and may never go.   —LISA RANDALL

Somebody else may have my rapturous glance at the
archangels. The springing of the yellow line of morning
out of the misty deep of dawn, is glory enough for me.

—ZORA NEALE HURSTON

There is grandeur in this view of life, with its several
powers, having been originally breathed into a few
forms or into one; and that, whilst this planet has gone
cycling on according to the fixed law of gravity, from so

simple a beginning endless forms most beautiful and most wonderful have been, and are being, evolved.

—CHARLES DARWIN

I asked him the most important question that I think you could ask—if he had ever seen *Caddyshack*.

—JESSE VENTURA, on his conversation with the Dalai Lama

A man is a very small thing and the night is very large and full of wonders.

—LORD DUNSANY, *Plays of God and Men*

The term supernatural is unintelligible to me. But on the other hand, nature itself seems so wonderful that I don't feel a hunger [f]or any concept beyond it.

—OLIVER SACKS

This is what non-scientists don't know, and this is what scientists are too bashful to talk about publicly, at least until they grow old enough to become shameless. Science at its highest level is ultimately the organization of, the systematic pursuit of, and the enjoyment of wonder, awe, and mystery.

—ABRAHAM MASLOW

As our eyes grow accustomed to sight they become armored against wonder.
—LEONARD COHEN, *The Favourite Game*

Life is not to have fun—it is to suffer, be enchanted, be amazed.
—KAREL ČAPEK (attributed)

It doesn't matter to me if you call it God or the cosmos. We're all talking about the same thing, whether it's religious people or New Age spiritual people or Buddhists or scientists. We're all talking about having a sense of awe and wonder at something grander than ourselves.
—MICHAEL SHERMER

Philosophy begins in wonder. And, at the end, when philosophic thought has done its best, the wonder remains.
—ALFRED NORTH WHITEHEAD

Wonder is what the philosopher endures most; for there is no other beginning of philosophy than this.
—PLATO

From the sublime to the ridiculous is but a step.
—NAPOLEON BONAPARTE

The world is a stunningly interesting and glorious place at every scale. And the awe that one can experience because one understands something about how the parts are put together is I think far greater than the sort of awe of incomprehension. —DANIEL DENNETT

Find something that isn't a miracle, you'll have cause to wonder then. —LAURENCE HOUSMAN

Work

Work is the only good thing.   —John Steinbeck

The life of leisure doesn't give us a moment's rest.
                                   —James Merrill

To apply oneself to great inventions, starting from the smallest beginnings, is no task for ordinary minds; to divine that wonderful arts lie hid behind trivial and childish things is a conception for superhuman talents.
                                   —Galileo Galilei

What you have to do now is work. There's no right way to start.   —Anna Held Audette

Most people spend the greatest part of their time working in order to live, and what little freedom remains so fills them with fear that they seek out any and every means to be rid of it.
                    —Johann Wolfgang von Goethe,
                    The Sorrows of Young Werther

What man actually needs is not some tension-less state but rather the striving and struggling for some goal worthy of him.
—VIKTOR FRANKL

Labor is the only prayer that Nature answers; it is the only prayer that deserves an answer—good, honest, noble work.
—ROBERT G. INGERSOLL

Author's Note

A portion of the proceeds of this book will be donated to the humanitarian medical aid organization Doctors Without Borders, whose mission is to "provide assistance to populations in distress, to victims of natural or man-made disasters and to victims of armed conflict, irrespective of race, religion, creed, or political convictions."

For more information about Doctors Without Borders, please visit www.doctorswithoutborders.org.

SOURCES

Perhaps you've seen the following quotation online, next to a photo of the sixteenth president of the United States:

> "Don't believe everything you read on the Internet."
> —Abraham Lincoln

As this joke suggests, many of the quotations one finds online are improperly attributed, only partially accurate, or wholly invented. The same is often true of quotation books. But not, I hope, this one.

I have done my best to track down primary source material for every quotation in this book. I deleted dozens of delightful quotations from the final text when I was unable to provide adequate evidence of their attribution. In order to avoid overwhelming the final book with hundreds of pages of citations, the full text of footnotes for *The Inspirational Atheist* can be found on my Web site, www.BuzzyJackson.com.

Because, as Abraham Lincoln actually said:

"I believe it is an established maxim in morals that he who makes an assertion without knowing whether it is true or false, is guilty of falsehood; and the accidental truth of the assertion, does not justify or excuse him."

—Abraham Lincoln, letter to the editor of the *Illinois Gazette*,

August 11, 1846

ACKNOWLEDGMENTS

To the friends and family who supported the idea and writing of this book, suggested ideas and quotations for inclusion in it, helped with research, and otherwise "got it" from the start, thank you: Ben Kirshner, Jackson Kirshner, Gary Morris, Becky Cole, Ruth Jackson Hall, Jon A. Jackson, Devin Jackson, Keith Hall, Kathryn Kirshner, Lewis Kirshner, Dawn Skorczewski, Delight and Paul Dodyk, the extended Meschery family, Phebe and Adam Kiryk, Micaela and Eric Schulz, Greg Duncan, Tania Schoennagel and Steve Leovy, Nat Gleason, Noelle Colome, Will Richardson, Michael Patterson, Valerie Goodman, Mollie Doyle, Robert Saunders, Bethy Leonardi, Michelle Theall, Hannah Nordhaus, Rachel Weaver, Radha Marcum, Rachel Odell Walker, Nancy Coulter-Parker, Garson O'Toole (aka The Quote Investigator), Staci Rosenthal, Kathleen Kleidermacher, Samantha Russo, and Rose-Anne and Brandan Reynolds.